Diary of a Gay Priest

The Tightrope Walker

Diary of a Gay Priest

The Tightrope Walker

Malcolm Johnson

CHRISTIAN
ALTERNATIVE

Winchester, UK
Washington, USA

First published by Christian Alternative Books, 2013
Christian Alternative Books is an imprint of John Hunt Publishing Ltd.,
Laurel House, Station Approach,
Alresford, Hants, SO24 9JH, UK
office1@jhpbooks.net
www.johnhuntpublishing.com
www.christian-alternative.com

For distributor details and how to order please visit the 'Ordering' section on our website.

Text copyright: Malcolm Arthur Johnson 2013

ISBN: 978 1 78279 002 0

A CIP catalogue record for this book is available from the British Library.

Design: Stuart Davies
Cover Photograph: The Tightrope Walker by David Shenton, 1994.

Printed in the USA by Edwards Brothers Malloy

We operate a distinctive and ethical publishing philosophy in all
areas of our business, from our global network of authors to
production and worldwide distribution.

CONTENTS

For Robert

Acknowledgements

My sincere thanks to my friends Kevin Kelly and Paul Thurtle for helping me with their computer skills and photography. My editors have been painstakingly helpful in preparing this book and I am grateful. David Shenton has allowed me to use his cartoon of me so thanks also to him.

A few names and situations have been changed
to protect privacy.

Introduction

I realised that I was gay when I was eight, about four years before I decided to be a priest. At school and parties I was very attracted physically to boys and never girls. It was wartime, and having been evacuated from our house in Great Yarmouth, Norfolk, we were living in Acle, a tiny village between Norwich and Great Yarmouth. Our home was destroyed soon after we left, and my grandmother's house also in Yarmouth disappeared a fortnight later whilst she was safely in a communal shelter, although her dog escaped from the house and found her in the shelter. I remember little of it. Until we rented a house of our own we all lived with my great aunt Agatha – hair swept back into a bun, lanky and slightly dotty. Unlike Bertie Wooster's aunt, she was child friendly, and even forgave me when I picked her prize carnations and gave them to her as a present. Her huge garden with its herbaceous borders, rose garden, meadows for horses and smelly lake was a rural idyll, and in my imagination I can still visit the hen houses to collect eggs and go into the kitchen garden to pick redcurrants, gooseberries, Victoria plums and strawberries. The motor house contained an ancient Morris in which Uncle Jimmy travelled to Yarmouth every day to keep an eye on his bakery and shops. He tolerated me until I won at cards (Newmarket) after dinner – 'It's time that boy was in bed.'

In 1940 aged four I was sitting outside the Queen's Head one Sunday morning waiting for my parents and their American army friends (GIs) to emerge when Albert the gardener took me to a hen house and showed me how to wring a chicken's neck. 'Now you do it,' so I did, then put the poor thing into a bucket and took it to my parents who were horrified. So was I. Later in my life there were several bishops I would have enjoyed doing that to.

Aged 5½, I started at Acle village school on 13 April 1942 and soon had a 'Just William' gang of boys, all of whom being sons of farm labourers had broad Norfolk accents. After school we roamed the fields, and one day Peter, slightly younger than me, had an accident. I put him in a wheelbarrow and when I got back to our bungalow I threw open the door and yelled, 'Peter's shat his pants.' My mother gave me 'the look' because she was entertaining some ladies, and told me to wheel him to his own house which I did. Peter had a friend aged 10 who was tough, good looking and very handsome. I would be cheeky to him which meant that he would wrestle me to the ground, which was sheer bliss to me. When I saw his mother in the baker's shop I was terrified that somehow she knew about this. War was raging and occasionally bombs dropped nearby.

We moved back to Yarmouth after the war when I was nine, and I was sent to a Roman Catholic convent school my mother had attended where I caught Christianity from the Irish nuns who wore the old style gear with wimples which had white starched frames around their faces. I adored them, and they taught me to pray and sing hymns.[1] My mother couldn't understand it, because at the same school the sadistic sisters had made her kneel on a grating when she was naughty. My parents now decided I needed toughening up, so after a year sent me to a prep school (Duncan House) in the town where I became a weekly boarder. It seemed odd to me because I could have walked to school each day, and sometimes I would forlornly return to the house but never go in. After two years the school transferred to Scratby, a small village near Yarmouth, and the Alastair Sim look-a-like local vicar Leonard Tillett came in to teach us religious knowledge. He invited me to his vicarage in Ormesby where he lived in refined poverty with his wife, adopted daughter and Miss Teasdel, the lodger. Seeing him at work I decided I wanted to be a priest and told him so. He befriended and encouraged me. On Sundays I went alone to St Peter's church, Great Yarmouth where the reredos and font were given in memory of my great-grandparents. No one spoke to me, and I didn't understand a word of the vicar's sermons. There was no incense, but another fragrance filled the air from fur coats, hence I later called the service 'Mothball Matins'. We would emerge from this dismal service looking as though we had been at a memorial service for God.

At school in 1947 when I was eleven I was in the queue for cocoa before we got into our ice-cold sheets, when we were all asked what we wanted to be when we grew up. My pious reply 'I am going to be a parson' brought shrieks of laughter from the Head's wife, and beating the ladle on the table she told all the boys what I had said. I'm not sure I ever forgave her. My diary began that year although entries were sparse – 'cold today' or 'more electricity cuts' etc.

Sex among the boarders was taken for granted, and a look-out would be posted each evening at the dormitory door after lights out. I enjoyed the fumbling mutual masturbation, and no one ever got caught. The best fun was getting into a cupboard with a boy who was captain of rugby and victor ludorum. I had no idea what that meant, so cheekily would call him Victor to get him to wrestle me to the floor. At this time I had my first European holiday, and when we were in Paris whilst the Aged Parents (both 40) went to the Folies Bergère I was left in the care of the hotel manager who promptly took me round the gay nightclubs and swore me to secrecy. When we returned a year later I was told that he had committed suicide.

In 1950 my parents gave me the option of staying on at my prep school or going to a public school, so, as I had no idea what to do, I wrote to the Agony Aunt of *Woman and Home*. I can't remember her reply; but aged 14, I was transferred to Framlingham College[2] which was then an eleventh rate boarding school in Suffolk, where the prefects ran the place once lessons ended and the teachers had gone home. The result was bullying and cruelty on a grand scale laced with sex. Framlingham was not the only school where this happened because there was a respected tradition in public schools which said that after lessons were over, boys should govern themselves according to their own laws. In the 1950s and earlier they chose the law of the jungle, and this was defended by the masters who considered that the boys were being prepared for later life where toughness and endurance were needed. For the first three years I hated the place – as did Sir Alfred Munnings, according to his memoirs. When I became a prefect with a study of my own, life began to improve. I was prepared for confirmation in my first year by the sadistic chaplain, Rupert Kneese, who made me learn the catechism by heart, and thumped me with his glasses case or a ruler if I got the answers wrong. He also did a good line in a Chinese cheek-twisting torture. On our first meeting in his tobacco-stained study, he asked my name – 'Malcolm Johnson, sir.' He replied, 'I don't want to know your Christian name, boy.' His eyes went in different directions so if in class he said, 'Stand up, boy,' two boys stood up. He was more interested in rifle shooting than religion.

Despite this I took Christianity very seriously, was confirmed and served at the early communion service. When term ended and I went home the Yarmouth vicar,[3] tipped off by my step-grandmother (my real grandma had died in 1921 when Father was 11), took me into the vestry, told me to kneel and prayed over me – may I be worthy of my great family, and follow in the footsteps of my grandfather. This was a little surprising because he, a churchwarden, married a divorcée and when he was refused a church wedding never darkened the doors again. My moment of fame at Framlingham was to star as Titania in *A Midsummer Night's Dream* produced in the Castle. I wore a floor-length diaphanous dress which was very embarrassing because I was the only fairy with hairy legs. I left school in 1955 with everyone except my parents knowing that I wanted to be ordained; Father expected me to go into the family firm of clothing manufacturers, which had been founded around 1860.

I served in the Royal Norfolk Regiment as a subaltern for my National Service 1955–7, and had no sex whatsoever. I hoped that a fellow officer, who had also been at Framlingham where we had regular sex, might oblige, but unfortunately for me he was engaged shortly afterwards. As a private I served my basic training at Britannia Barracks in Norwich, and on the first night I heard the man in the next bed crying presumably from homesickness. He was a tough farm labourer so I kept quiet about it. My officer training was at Eaton Hall, the huge Victorian pile near Chester. Subsequently demolished it was the home of the Duke of Westminster; one Duchess had described it as more of a town than a house. It had acres of garden which I enjoyed.

I served in Cyprus where the Greek islanders wanted ENOSIS – union with Greece – and had formed a terrorist organisation, EOKA, led by General Grivas. In the Officers' Mess one evening I was given a roasting by a fellow officer for stating conservative views on homosexuality – 'Fancy you of all people saying that.' I was horrified and rushed back to my room. Had he seen through my façade, and realised the true story? I went to bed sick and apprehensive. The next morning I

I served as an officer in the Royal Norfolk Regiment 1955-57.

realised what he had meant. Everyone knew I was going to be ordained so it surprised him to hear such views mouthed by me. I was ashamed.

I enjoyed Cyprus although it was a dangerous place and several members of the regiment were killed. Part of our duties was to patrol the Limassol streets trying to catch pamphlet throwers, but bored by this I twice asked my driver to take me to local monasteries where, removing my pistol, I would explain to the monks that I was to be ordained, and would like to look round. Always they agreed and gave me tiny cups of coffee. I later realised how foolish this was because Grivas in his diaries revealed that he often hid in monasteries.

During leave, before joining the regiment in Germany, I went

to St John's Theological College, Durham for an interview with the Principal, Canon Higginbotham. After a friendly chat he asked if I had any questions. I said, 'Does the college have a bar?' He replied, 'Gracious no, is that a problem?' Afterwards I raced across Palace Green to University College in the Castle, pulled the bell and explained that I needed an interview. The gatekeeper phoned the Senior Tutor who saw me almost immediately, and offered me a place two

My parents, Molly and Russell, at my Graduation in Durham, 1960.

weeks later for 1957. Selwyn, Cambridge had agreed to have me in 1958 but I didn't want to wait a year.

In Germany we lived in a former Nazi officers' mess in Iserlohn. I did not much care for manoeuvres, which were held all over the country, and I found it hard to take them seriously. Once 'standing to' at dawn with my platoon in a trench I spotted some edible mushrooms, so I wormed my way over to them and collected them in my tin hat. Unfortunately the Colonel had his binoculars trained on our lines and a stormy tirade came over the radio asking who the 'Bloody Fool' was. We said that we had no idea, and Colonel Brinkley unknowingly enjoyed them later for breakfast.

I went up to Durham and led a celibate life for three years. My college, known as Castle, only had around 250 students, all men. There were five other colleges for men, and three for women. Colleges in Newcastle were also part of the university, but we in Durham only had 1,500 students[4] so it was easy to know a good proportion of them, particularly as I became President of the Student Christian Movement which had a large membership. Durham was a very religious place with two theological colleges and an institution to train women church workers. It was rumoured that their chaplain had told them that if they had sexy thoughts they should clean their shoes, so all the hearty heterosexual men looked to see who had the cleanest shoes. I immersed myself in churchy organisations, and for fun, as I was only nine stone, I coxed the College and then the University boat. We usually rowed in fours on the Wear which winds its way around the huge rock on which the Cathedral and castle stand, and is a nightmare to coxes because of its bridges and bends. Our eights trained on the Tyne at Newcastle. Durham Cathedral was a constant inspiration to me, and most days I would pray there.

On 9 September 1958, the day after my 22nd birthday, I went to see the patrician Bishop of Norwich, Percy Herbert, at his Palace next to the Cathedral to discuss the possibility of my training as a priest, doing a curacy, then whilst working at Johnson's, the family firm, caring for a small parish near Yarmouth. Tall, aristocratic with grey bushy eyebrows, he listened attentively, then said, 'It's a marvellous idea but quite impossible because we don't have worker priests in the Church of England except for teachers.' I must choose between the two careers, and he offered to come and talk to my father. I could imagine what my father would say if the Provincial Grand Master of the Freemasons walked into his office, so said that I'd think it over. Father was not religious, and reckoned that the three attendances each Sunday he had endured as a child gave him a season ticket for life. Once when the vicar called he said, 'There's no one at home.' 'Well, you are at home,' said Gilbert Thurlow.

I liked Percy Herbert enormously because he took me seriously. His father had been one of Queen Victoria's generals,[5] and he had been Bishop of Blackburn for 15 years before coming to Norwich in 1942. Whilst at Durham I came south to attend the enthronement of his successor, Launcelot Fleming. Percy, still Clerk of the Closet,[6] was present when the new bishop went to Buckingham Palace to kiss hands. The Queen turned to Percy and asked how many parishes there were in the Norwich diocese. 'Can't say, Ma'am; never counted.' The enthronement was grand opera, but my resolve to be ordained faltered slightly when I saw the robed rustic clergy of the Dead See arrive with straw coming out of their ears – around 400 of them from 628 churches. Sixty-nine parishes have a population of less than 100 and 87 have less than 1,000, and 61 benefices are vacant. Did I really want to be part of all this? Yes, I did, so in September 1958 I went to the selection board at Farnham Castle to see if I should be ordained. The process was similar to my officer selection board except that there was no obstacle course over pews and pulpits. Whilst there I met a young man, Michael Marshall, and we went into town for a late night drink but we got locked out so had to throw stones at a window so someone would let us in. Both of us had already been accepted by Cuddesdon theological college and the lock-out didn't affect our chances, because on the 20th Percy wrote to say I had passed. Michael had too.

At Cuddesdon (1960–2) I was celibate and tried to ignore my homosexual feelings as, I suspect, did many of the other students. The subject was rarely mentioned, but I did fall in love with a sun-tanned, hairy Australian from Cairns in Queensland. We couldn't understand why he showered every day because he didn't look dirty, and he thought us English with our weekly bath night were a filthy lot. Jim Warner came to stay with me in the holidays and we had a warm non-physical friendship, although I always hoped for more. After a curacy in Poplar he returned to Queensland and eventually became a college Principal. When he was dying from an AIDS-related illness in 1993 I wrote to him telling him the whole story, and he replied saying that he had been 'a silly goose' in those days, and how much I had meant to him. After his death his partner, Chris, sent me the short biography prepared by friends in which Chris was not mentioned.

Cuddesdon is in the depths of the Oxfordshire countryside and was a monastic place in 1960, so when my Durham friend, Juliet Dearmer, turned up unexpectedly to see me one Wednesday afternoon she was told that women were only allowed in the college for Sunday tea. I was out for a walk, so eventually she was put in the vicarage music room. After a while a head came round the door, and she was asked if she needed a lavatory. She said no, and the student said, 'Oh good, because I don't know which one you could use.'

The ordered life at Cuddesdon suited me and, being devout, I made my confession regularly. The deadly sins didn't get a look in because my shopping list of sins was dominated by my attraction to men, and having them in mind when I masturbated. Confessors reacted differently, and a Kelham[7] Father told me to wash my hands when these thoughts appeared so I had the cleanest hands in Christendom. Robert Runcie, the Principal, arranged my curacy to be at St Mark Portsea which was a large parish of 25,000 staffed by a vicar and eight curates, four of whom, including me, lived in the clergy house.

At Portsmouth I tried unsuccessfully to deal with my problems by working all hours, but after a year I decided I needed help, so I went to see Chad Varah,[8] founder of the Samaritans, in his eyrie in the tower of St Stephen Walbrook in the City of London. He listened attentively, asked questions, then suggested that as I was obviously frightened of women he would arrange for a lady he knew to take me to parties etc in London. I was horrified, and ran up Cheapside to pray and cry in St Paul's. However, after another year I was so depressed and anxious that I returned to talk with him again. This time he suggested I see a psychotherapist, so I began to see Mrs Rowena Phillips, elegant, plump and upper class, twice a week. She had been analysed by Emma Jung in Zurich, and was also one of the founding members of the British Association of Psychotherapists.

On Mondays I would drive from Portsmouth to her home near Guildford, and on Thursday I went by train to London to see her in Queen Anne Street. I would lie on a couch with her sitting behind me smoking a cigarette. She gave me a special rate of £3 per week and must have loosened up something because I began to have sex with men for the first time in eight years. On Thursdays, after our session, I would go to All Saints Margaret Street for Evensong sung by the well-drilled boy choristers presided over by their vicar, Fr Kenneth Ross or his curate, Fr John Gaskell,[9] who then appeared to me as a frightening, button-upped man in a soutane and cotta. The music in the darkened Gothic church was sublime and acted as balm after my time on the couch. Supper followed, and then I picked up a rent boy in Piccadilly for £3 and took him to my Bayswater hotel, which also cost £3. I am not proud of this era of my life but I was desperate – not just for sex but for love. Since then I have had a distaste and disgust of paying for sex which my gay friends cannot understand, telling me that if you pay for a meal you can also pay for sex, and, anyway, you usually get exactly what you want. One friend says that sex should be available on the National Health.

Needless to say, I did not mention any of this to the Jung Lady whose agenda was to make me heterosexual. I lay on her couch passively waiting for something to happen. She once suggested a course of LSD[10] which sounded a good idea, but a friend told me that it rips the unconscious open with a tin opener. So after an initial consultation with Dr Henry of the Marlborough Day Hospital in his white-tiled room I refused; although I did agree to go to a fortnightly group session enabled by Paul de Berker, who sat with us ten damaged people, and with hooded eyes made the occasional fatuous remark: 'Malcolm, you seem to be avoiding Jean's eyes.' Of course I was. The disadvantage of the ninety-minute group was that I had to wait longer for the fun in the hotel. My diary does not mention this, but the occasional note MM betrays what we got up to. I had to tell my vicar, Peter May, about these two counselling sessions because I only had one day off each week. I swore him to secrecy using the seal of the confessional, so I was a little surprised when a year later the Bishop asked me how the therapy was going.

I was kept busy running the huge Sunday Schools and youth clubs. I thank God that I have never been sexually attracted to teenagers, so there was no danger for me when they wrestled with me or jumped all over me. I think that I was probably an affectionate older brother – I was only 27 – but I was lonely and it showed. I needed someone to love me. Then everything changed because on the day before I left Portsmouth in 1967 to go to be a university chaplain in London, Susan rang the clergy house doorbell. She was the only woman I had taken out in Durham, and I liked her immensely. She told me that she had been a nun for five years and was now a nurse at St Thomas' Hospital in London, had looked me up in Crockford's, and travelled by train to see me again. It seemed that God had spoken and given me a sign, so Susan and I agreed to meet in London which we did. For years I had prayed for a wife and now God had delivered one on the doorstep. At one of our meetings I explained my problems, and she, a devout Christian, thought that we could beat this homosexual thing together. Susan and I met regularly in London when I was at the Queen Mary College Chaplaincy, going to meals and the theatre; then we married 18 months later in December 1968.

Five days before the wedding we went to the College Christmas Ball, and I spent much time staring at Richard who lived in one of the six chaplaincy rooms. Fair, bronzed and fit he looked superb as he danced with his girlfriend. Always he had been affectionate with me and often provoked me to a wrestling match so that I could feel his body next to mine. He once knocked me out, and when I came to he was cuddling me on the floor. What rapture. I once told him that I loved him, did it worry him? 'Not at all; if you said you hated me then I would be worried.' I told Susan I wanted to leave the Ball, so we returned to the chaplaincy where I broke down. How could we go ahead with the wedding if I felt like this? How could we not? The guests would be arriving in five days' time, the reception was arranged, and most of the gifts had already arrived. She felt we must go ahead, and I agreed. The marriage was a dismal flop, fiasco and failure. I could not satisfy her physically, and after a great deal of pain for us, our families and friends, an annulment was given. The diary describes very little of this; it was too painful.

Just after we agreed to part I met Robert Wilson who had been at an Albany Trust lecture in the City University where he was studying engineering. The subject of the talk was homosexuality, and he thought the lecturer, Fr Fabian Cowper, very handsome, so next day asked Doreen Cordell, the Trust's counsellor, if he might see him. 'He is Roman Catholic and you are an Anglican,' he was told, 'so you have to go and see Malcolm Johnson.' Thank God he did, because we have now been together 43 years. This diary is not sexually explicit, but we soon had to work out what we thought about physical faithfulness. After a bout of faithfulness we soon realised that most male gay couples need and want sex outside their relationship, and we came to an arrangement and agreement. It might be different for lesbians, I really don't know. Some couples tell each other every detail, and that might turn them on; some couples prefer not to tell each other anything, and others tell what they think the partner can cope with. I have always thought that just as there is a sexual spectrum from extreme hetero to extreme homo (and most of us are somewhere in between) so there is a spectrum between those who never stop thinking about sex and those who never start. Again, most of us are somewhere in the middle.

After a while Robert and I laid down certain ground rules which have lasted till today. If one of us asks for details he will be told; above all there should be no involvement with someone else which might lead to an affair. What people think or might say is of no relevance to us. In my twenties I was hung up on sexual sins, and my confessions were dominated and obsessed by them. Then I realised that consensual sex between men is not sinful if it causes no pain or hurt to each other or other people. I would not presume to say if this applies to heterosexuals. I have always known that only a few gay men are celibate, and a tiny number of male couples are physically faithful to each other. I remember preaching at a Cambridge College chapel and at dinner afterwards the chaplain and his partner took me to task for saying this, and promised me they were committed solely to each other. Three years later one of them told me that this was certainly not true, but he couldn't say so at the time.

I have dropped six of the seven veils in the diary.

Diary

I never travel without my diary. One should always have something sensational to read on the train.
Oscar Wilde

17 June 1962. In Portsmouth Cathedral my mother was very apprehensive because Fr Dennis, the Franciscan preacher at my deaconing, said that we were to be branded today. I had no idea what he meant. Instead of fetching hot tongs she saw that hands were laid on me by Bryan Robin the retired Bishop of Adelaide.[11] As we processed out I remembered that as a student I had visited a man in the Radcliffe Infirmary, who when I told him that I was to be ordained told me, 'Mister, you won't do much.'

25 June 1962. At my first staff meeting the vicar said that the Mother's Union wanted a talk: 'A day in the life of a parson'. 'Malcolm, you've been here seven days, so go and describe one of them.' The days are certainly very full – communion, matins and meditation in the morning then work through the day, mainly visiting the 1,000 homes in my area of the parish, and tramping over every inch of the cemeteries. Four of us live in the clergy house and Pricey, our cockney housekeeper, spoils us; on six days each week we have a cooked breakfast, lunch and high tea.

6 September 1962. The previous priest in my area of the parish is Nicolas Stacey who had been an Olympic runner and friend of Chris Chataway, Roger Bannister etc. Every house I visit I am told about him, which is tiresome, but he must have run fast to visit all these families.

1 August 1962. I have been accepted by Durham University to study for an MA and write a thesis on Bishop Charles James Blomfield the reforming Bishop of London who invigorated the diocese 1829–56. He is a much neglected figure and I was intro-duced to him by John Brooks our Vice Principal at Cuddesdon –

one wit said that Cuddesdon is better known for its vices than its principals. So every Tuesday morning at 9am I go to 120 Balfour Road where one of our congregation, Mrs Purkiss, lets me use her front room to do my research until 1pm, when she and her friend Miss Davies usually provide me with a tasty lunch.

14 February 1963. My youth club's Valentine's Dance in our huge dilapidated Edwardian parish hall with 400 teenagers paying two shillings each to jump around to the band. Cuddesdon hardly prepared me for this, and, as the police kept calling in, I patrolled the hall all evening so there were no fights.

21 March 1963. My parents invited me to join them at the American Hotel in Amsterdam for a holiday. I've heard that the city is a meeting place for homosexuals, so on Sunday night I walked around the empty streets in the rain looking for a gay club, but couldn't find one. I desperately need love and sex. Going back to the hotel I looked out of the window at the canal and cried my heart out. When I return to England I must phone the Samaritans.

28 May 1963. Am at Cerne Abbas, the Franciscan friary, taking stock of my first year in the ministry, and I'm not sure I like what I see. It has been frantically busy so personal needs have been shoved into the background. Living a communal life with three others[12] in a clergy house is pleasant, but it lacks privacy and has not helped me grow as an individual. I have enjoyed my work, particularly visiting and getting to know (and I hope be trusted by) several generations of a family. My big problem is still my sexuality and every day I think about it. In some ways it hinders my work but strangely enough I don't pray about it. If only my homosexuality could be taken away. As well as the daily offices I only spend about ten minutes in prayer. What shall I do after Portsmouth? Become a Franciscan, go to New Guinea or back to Norfolk? I feel very lonely and need a wife and children.

9 June 1963. I am made a priest by Bishop John Phillips of Portsmouth who says he will see me at any time on any subject

except how terrible the vicar is. In fact Canon Peter May is a gentle academic who lets us get on with our work without interfering. I have seen him for an hour each week which has been very useful. My guess is that he and his wife Elizabeth would prefer to be back in Calcutta where he was Principal of Bishop's College. I also think that he lives in the shadow of his predecessors, Gerald Ellison and Christopher Pepys, both of whom became bishops, and who still have fan clubs here. The ordination is in St Mark's so all *my* fan club are there. Roger Royle and James Buckett, a schoolmaster, are the other priests, and as Roger loves to be the centre of attention I seat him behind a huge display of white lilac. I admire him enormously and we can laugh about the lilac.

22 November 1963. I am secretary of the Deanery Missionary committee and the other members have left it to me to organise today's Missionary Rally in the Guildhall with an audience of around 800. Just after it had started the manager came to me and said that there was some terrible news. I went outside, and he said that President Kennedy had been shot and they were unsure whether he would live. I didn't know what to do, but eventually went on to the stage during a hymn and told the Bishop. He asked me to verify it and let the proceedings carry on, but after I later passed him a note saying it was true he asked everyone to stand for special prayers. Johnson's initiative tests when he was a subaltern came to his aid tonight.

9 June 1964: Roger Royle and I have a friendly rivalry about our Sunday Schools. Last Lent he got more children by having Daleks walking through the streets as adverts, defeating my 'Johnny and the Six Dreadful Giants' (even though one masked giant knocked herself out walking into a closed door).

10 August 1964. I am very unpopular. Yesterday the 6–12 year olds in our Sunday school travelled to Southampton Zoo with their teachers in three double-decker buses for their annual outing with me in charge. It was very hot, so when we left the zoo

a little girl tugged my sleeve and said, 'May we paddle?' We had an hour to spare so I said yes. 'WE CAN PADDLE!' she shouted, and all the children removed most of their clothing and jumped in the three pools outside the gates of the zoo. The teachers came rushing up – 'What have you done? How can we dry them when there are no towels?' I hit on the idea of making the boys and girls run round the edges of the pools so they soon dried out, but then no one could find where they had left their clothes...

On our return to Portsmouth we discovered that we had left ten year old Jake Silverton at the zoo. 'I thought he was on your bus.' 'No, I thought he was on your bus.' I phoned the zoo and found that he had given himself up, and had been taken to the local police station. 'For God sake come and get him, he's wrecking the place,' said the station sergeant, so with fear and apprehension I first went to see his mum – 'Don't worry, Father, he's always getting lost' – then I drove at breakneck speed in my half-timbered Morris traveller to Southampton.

31 August 1964. Justin Banbury, one of my closest Cuddesdon friends, has died in a car crash and I am absolutely devastated. I would stay with him and his parents in Ealing, and we have met regularly since ordination because he is a curate at King's Lynn. It is a terrible loss as he was fiercely intelligent, charming and very popular. I wrote to his mother today and said that quite sincerely I wished it had been me who died. I meant it, as there doesn't seem much of a future for me.

1 September 1964. I have been given an MA from Durham for my thesis on Bishop Blomfield, so can now sport a purple silk hood.

7 September 1964. I am a terrible coward and cannot face Justin's funeral as I am so upset and I wouldn't want to meet his vicar, Eric Turnbull, who Justin heartily disliked. Justin has recently married, but I gather no child is on the way. He is one of the few healthily hetero men that I didn't fancy but was very close to.

22 October 1964. Another of my star-studded Missionary Rallies. This time Archbishop Michael Ramsey addresses 1,800 people in the Guildhall, and afterwards he kindly remembers partnering me at Cuddesdon in a game of croquet. He is the most vicious player I have ever met, knocking our opponents' balls into the flower beds with great zest. We won easily.

1 May 1965. Mrs Phillips, my therapist, the Jung Lady, is horrified that I am considering having a dog, and says that it would obviously be a substitute for a lover, so I straightway go out and buy one. I drove to the Petersfield kennels, and am now the proud possessor of an adorable black and white cocker spaniel puppy, Ben. He is very aristocratic so his kennel name will be Cosmo Cochise in memory of Cosmo Cantuar.[14] The others in the Clergy House have accepted him despite the puddles.

8 May 1965. The Provost of Portsmouth Cathedral, Eric Porter Goff[15] who is an autocratic, arrogant bully, wants the diocese to raise £350,000 to extend the Cathedral, and today on behalf of 25 junior clergy I made a speech at the Diocesan Conference attacking the plan and suggesting that the huge St Mary Portsea become the cathedral. I got much support and the project is condemned 117–109 with 12 abstentions. The Bishop who strongly supports the project is furious, and the Provost said to my vicar, 'Can't you keep your young men in order?' The Archdeacon commented, 'Malcolm looks so meek, but he obviously isn't.'[16]

1 October 1965. Canon HEW Turner, my tutor at Durham, writes to tell me, 'You are not forgotten in Durham. I remember so vividly your work for SCM and am not unmindful of a very respectable MA thesis for which I was one of the examiners.' He asks if I would like to be chaplain of my College. I have already turned down two offers from the London University Chaplaincy so with regret say no again. I am not ready to leave yet.

24 October 1965. Our vicar is in Wilmington, Delaware in the

States, and under the exchange plan we have Lloyd Gressle,[13] the Dean of the Anglican cathedral there, as our vicar for 12 months. Last Sunday, his first here, all went well except before the Parish Eucharist he wandered round the congregation clad in chasuble greeting everyone. At Evensong, using our old prayer book, he prayed devoutly for 'King Edward, Queen Alexandra, George, Prince of Wales...' so afterwards I explained his mistake, and he said, 'Perhaps the guy needs our prayers.' I like him and his wife; they are a breath of fresh air after our earnest old owl Peter May.

15 January 1966. One of the Jung Lady's bright ideas is that I should mix more with healthy heterosexuals of my own age, and last month she encouraged me to go skiing with a party of young people. So I have just spent ten days in Sölden, Austria with some young nurses, teachers etc who had advertised for others to join them. I have tried to be hearty, but hid the fact that I am a priest and obviously did not mention homosexuality. What an odd time, the highlights of which were the meals après ski and looking at the devastatingly handsome young instructor. Bronzed and fit, he hit the nail on the head by telling me I need to use my 'boody' more.

3 April 1966. Last evening was an adventure. A young woman who is taking too much interest in me invited me to spend an evening with her parents. I arrived at 7.30 and was given a thimble of sherry, but by 8.45 there was no sign of supper so I got up, said I had a hospital visit to do and left. This morning she appeared on the clergy house doorstep and thrust a paper bag into my hands – 'This is last night's meal.'

6 September 1966. I very much enjoy parish visiting but it has its dangers. I went to tea today with an elderly lady whose eyesight is bad and was given seed cake with mould on, so I had to transfer it to my pocket. A mouse walked across the floor presumably hoping for a share. Five minutes later it walked back again. I decided not to tell her.

20 October 1966. I have never played football in my life, but

am now a football manager and talk authoritatively about the game. Today I was interviewed by the *Church Times*. Eighteen months ago I assembled a team from our youth club, but the first game was a disaster. Our only goal was greeted by 'offside' from our slick tangerine-shirted opponents. 'Definitely not,' our linesman told the referee. I sidled over and asked him if he knew the rules: 'Of course not, but I wasn't going to tell him.' From there it was success all the way, and we now field three 12 to 15 teams every Sunday, and an outside team have asked me to manage them. I begged enough money from the congregation to buy jerseys, and the boys chose black with white collars so they look like a team of curates. I spend a lot of time bluffing so that during matches when other managers in the league come to talk tactics I tell them I should move on to see how the other teams are doing. Most of the 41 teenagers involved come to our Sunday service, and all to the youth club.

21 October 1966. Again I organise the Missionary Rally in the Guildhall with cast of thousands – 60 teenagers in a Pageant and around 300 in the choir on stage. The hall was full including the balcony and it has involved hours of work, but no one thanked me; John Phillips, the Bishop, hardly spoke to me. Why am I bothered? Looking for a father figure perhaps?

30 October 1966. Interview with Gordon Phillips the Senior Chaplain of the London University team. Am I suitable to be a college chaplain? I hardly spoke a word during the hour that he gave me. Fr Benedict Green, who had been his curate at Northolt, says that he 'combines formidable dialectical ability, Welsh eloquence, catholic conviction, left-wing politics, wide-ranging cultural enthusiasms and a lifetime's preoccupation with the nature of the act of faith.' I turned down a chaplaincy at Durham University because it would be too cosy, but this is a different kettle of fish, and I accept Fr Gordon's offer. All the London colleges except King's have chaplains attached who officially have no standing because when Jeremy Bentham founded

dog each day around Victoria Park feeling depressed and guilty because I cannot return her love, and have no sexual feelings for her. She is moving into a flat in the West End. I am desolate.

9 August 1969. Yarmouth. Feeling devastated I asked my parents to come into the dining room. 'What's happened now?' asked Mother. After walking round the room I said that the last few months had been hell and my marriage has to end. Father did not want to know more, but after a long silence I told them that I am homosexual. 'Well, you didn't get it from my side of the family,' said Mother.

2 September 1969. Wearing my best suit I drive to Fulham Palace, park the car in the Tudor quadrangle, and ring the bell. The chaplain takes me down long corridors and into the Bishop of London's study. Robert Stopford[20], a fatherly pipe-smoking man not long from retirement, has no idea why I am there. I explain what has happened and offer my resignation. He listens intently then there is a long silence whilst I look up at the portrait of Bishop Blomfield above the fireplace. What *would* he have said? Then the Bishop refused to accept my resignation, saying that I had done nothing wrong; I have made a huge mistake. If I had been a parish priest he probably would have to move me, but a college chaplain lives a different life. He felt that the staff and students of the college would understand and probably not be very interested.

3 October 1969. A letter from the Bishop asks me to preach in St Paul's as one of his nominees. What an affirmation. He also asks me to go and see him again.

14 August 1970. Robert who is now living with me at Woodford enjoys riding so has persuaded me to go on a ten-day pony trekking holiday on Dartmoor. The others in the party are a mixed bag including a party of middle-aged lady telephonists from London, one of whom in twin set and pearls had trouble getting her horse to move. 'Come on, Fiona darling' became a catch phrase of the holiday. (Fiona was the horse.) Last evening

our hut began to shake violently, so we opened our door to find the handsome young warden of the centre having sex with one of the telephonists on the hall floor – not a very pleasant sight.

1 December 1970. The SK social group which I helped found two years ago at the Wychcroft conference has been a lifesaver for me. Robert and I go every Saturday evening taking any man I have 'interviewed' during the previous week, so that means I can introduce him to the 40 or so who are present. I never seem to turn anyone away because they come after an interview with Doreen Cordell, the Albany Trust's counsellor. Nearly all are professional men and several are clergy. When we first started we had a serious half hour with a talk and questions, but we soon ran out of topics. When we got to 'The gay world and the Virgin Mary' we knew it was time to stop. We now meet in the former school hall because membership has grown and the common room is too small. We have a stunningly boring handout in case the police or press raid us – along the lines that we three wonderful social workers wish to provide a space so that homosexual men can discuss their problems together. We left out the social slant as we might be accused of running a bawdy house where people meet for sex, and we did not mention the illegal bar. Recently we started dancing, and our members glide across the floor of the hall doing the Gay Gordons, and the last waltz is a time for VERY close dancing and partners have to be prised apart when it ends. The only rule we now have at SK is that if you are asked to dance you must accept because rejection is hurtful especially for our ancient members.

10 January 1971. A note from the lady who has moved into the flat above us in Woodford: 'I appreciate that you have had no one living above you up til (sic) now, but *please* could you now please be quieter in your bedroom late at night. I can hear everything that goes on and frankly I would rather get some sleep. Mrs Head.' What have we been up to?

18 January 1971. I speak in the Tower Hamlets Deanery debate

on homosexuality and am opposed by the evangelical vicar of Spitalfields, Eddy Stride, who has the air of a shop steward about him. His speech is dominated by the horror of sodomy, and he talks of 'the racked bodies' it produces, whatever that means. Lesbians must find this talk very odd. After the debate Eddy's lady worker collared me and said, 'You'll be condoning sex with animals next.' Eddy is a figure of fun, and I recently asked him to speak on pornography at one of our Sunday evening meetings at the Woodford Halls of Residence. After their ham tea the students have nothing to do so we usually get a packed house. Eddy ended his presentation by asking them if they would bother to go and see the film on show at the Mile End Odeon called *The Lustful Vicar*? A huge roar said: 'Yes.'[21]

10 April 1971. As usual I am helping with 'The University of the Streets' organised by the Student Christian Movement for students from all over England to learn about inner-city problems such as homelessness, drugs, poverty etc. I do a morning's session on homosexuality, and last night twelve members asked me to take them to a gay club. The Rehearsal in Archer Street, Soho is our favourite so, with Jo Purvis the owner's agreement, Robert and I took them there. It has men and women members and the basement is always packed and noisy. On the bus going home two tough rugger men said, 'I bet you were surprised when we danced closely together.' I was. 'We didn't want them to think we were watching the animals in the zoo.' I knew they were not gay so congratulated them on being so assured of their sexuality that they could dance.

15 May 1971. I had a good conversation at Fulham Palace with Bishop Stopford who asked some very searching questions about gay men and women. How do they see the Church? How do they cope with living secret lives? I felt he was very perceptive about the pain that is caused by the Church's attitude, and suggested that for my next job I would like to be a chaplain to the gay community, visiting the clubs and bars and getting involved with

the new groups being founded. I have already visited Gaylib and had been through their initiation talk before I was allowed into their meeting held in a Notting Gate church hall. The Bishop realises that many clergy are gay, and feels that a hidden ministry to them is also needed. He promised to think the matter over and see if he could help. I drove home feeling very supported and affirmed.

2 June 1971. Sir Harry Melville, Principal of the College, and his wife have been summoned to Windsor Castle for a sleepover, so I suggested that he ask the Queen for a painting of Queen Mary as we haven't got one. I remember seeing her at Sandringham when I was 12 and thinking that her face was enamelled which it probably was.

15 August 1971. We are staying with the Franciscans at Alnmouth and Brother Edward takes me aside and says that my place is in the First Order – 'You will be so lonely when you are old.' I ask what Robert would think of that. 'Oh, it won't last,' he says.

3 September 1971. I was summoned to the Principal's office. 'Now look what you've done,' he said pointing to a huge portrait of Queen Mary in a massive gilt frame. After dinner at Windsor when he was being shown early photos of the East End and the People's Palace now part of Queen Mary College, he had popped the question about the painting, and here it is. 'We have a large number in store, I'll send you one,' HM had told him. 'Where on earth can we put it?' he asks, so we toured the college and only find one wall large enough – in the Library.

2 February 1972. Gilbert Thurlow offers me the living of Morley St Botolph, Norfolk, which has two churches and 500 parishioners together with the chaplaincy of Wymondham College. I want to be in London so again say no.[22]

28 March–12 April 1972. Since 1968 I have every year been chaplain on a schoolchildren's cruise on SS *Uganda* or SS *Nevasa*. Around 900 children and 300 cabin passengers are on board with

the teachers forming the staff of this floating school – one teacher to 12 children. This year I flew to Venice then we cruised to Piraeus, Heraklion, Malta, Tangier and Lisbon. All I have to do – with the RC chaplain – is take the daily Assembly and the communion services. For the rest of the time I wander round the decks being nice to everyone. Attendances at communion vary, but this time we had a rough ride through the Bay of Biscay so of the 12 girls who started the early morning service six rushed out at the Gospel, two more at the consecration prayer, and only two were left at the end. The children are aged 12 to 15, but this time we had some older and tougher Canadians who won all the competitions and sports. Our kids got fed up, but got their revenge when I produced the concert on the last night. Some of the English boys dressed up in check shirts and in a Canadian accent sang the Monty Python song:

I'm a lumberjack and I'm OK...
I put on women's clothing and hang around in bars...
I wish I was a girlie just like my dear papa.

8 August 1972. Robert, Bishop of London, wonders if the Grosvenor Chapel might be 'a suitable base' for my specialised ministry. He is pondering how to finance it as publicity must be avoided. 'The work is very important and urgent,' he writes.

15 August 1972. Robert and I have little cash between us so we decide on a cheap four days' holiday at Bobby's Gay Guest House in Brighton. Last night was our first and only one because we have decided to leave – the room is damp and the place filthy. At breakfast this morning a distinguished-looking gent came in and said that he had been put in the communal room at the top of the house, and also would not be staying. When he arrived at 7pm yesterday he opened the bedroom door to find three fat, elderly men having sex. 'One who looked like a vicar stood up,' he said, 'and introduced the other two. We all shook hands and

then I fled.' From his description I guessed that the man was not a vicar but an organist of a London church, and sure enough the man walked in shortly afterwards.

13 October 1972. The family firm of clothing manufacturers, Johnson and Sons, has been sold and I am sad because if I had gone into it this probably need not have happened. The jobs of the 540-people workforce are safe and my father remains vice-chairman. He seems very phlegmatic about it, but I feel guilty. However, there is no way I could have survived as a gay man in Yarmouth.

9 March 1973. Robert writes again to say that he has not forgotten me and a decision needs to be made about my next sphere of work 'but it is extremely difficult to see where the specialist work you feel called to do can be based.' To make it a specialism on its own would be dangerous 'from many points of view but principally from your own position. Any thing like Troy Perry's separate denomination in America[23] would be disastrous. How would you react to be part of a team?' What a wise man! I tell him it is an excellent idea.

19 May 1973. Fr Harry Williams a Mirfield Father is taking a retreat at St Katharine's so, as I have been enormously helped by his books especially *Jesus and the Resurrection*, I ask to see him for some direction. His recent book shows that he has had psychotherapy, and several friends tell me that he is gay, so I was hoping for some help and advice. I was immensely disappointed; he continually referred to 'queers' and treated me with coldness and almost contempt, so I left feeling hurt, angry and depressed. I can only think that he dislikes my openness about the subject.

23 October 1973. Gerald Ellison, Bishop of Chester and the post-war vicar of my first parish, St Mark Portsea, is the new Bishop of London because +Robert has retired which saddens me as he has been so good to me.

2 February 1974. Out of the blue comes a letter from +Gerald asking if I would consider becoming rector of St Botolph Aldgate

in the City of London. I took two minutes to decide. It has a very tiny Sunday congregation ministered to by the staff of St Dunstan Stepney; a church infant/junior school next to it; and the crypt is divided between a club for Asian boys and an evening centre for the homeless. There is a verger, Peter, and a tiny Germanic lady worker Trudie Eulenburg who is abrupt and, as Bishop George Appleton a former rector observed, 'not everyone's cup of tea but a brand of her own.'

20 June 1974. I heard today that John Hester, the vicar of Soho, had congratulated the Bishop on my appointment saying, 'Now he can get on with his work.' 'What work?' asked the Bishop. John told him and it seems it has made no difference. Apparently Bishop Robert had a huge bonfire at Fulham and one of the files he burnt was mine, so Gerald knows very little about me except that I was a curate in his old Portsea parish, and that we both have a mutual interest in Bishop Blomfield.[24]

25 June 1974. My Induction as rector of St Botolph's. +Gerald gets angry because we start late, so I explain that I opened the lavatory door and a very drunk homeless man fell out who had to be escorted off the premises. There was a very large congregation and many robed clergy, Religious and readers. After the reception the Bishop commented on the large number of young men in the gallery and elsewhere. 'Your ministry in the College has obviously been effective.' I didn't tell him that term had ended and most undergraduates had gone home, so the men he saw were nearly all young gay friends of mine.

28 June 1974. My first Sunday service which is attended by nine people including my two churchwardens, Billy a teacher and Sonia a ward sister at the London Hospital, who sit either side of me in the sanctuary. How can I persuade them that their place is by the door to welcome everyone? I looked down the church and thought everyone including me looked odd.

9 September 1974. Aldgate rectory is in Purley, and I accepted the living on condition that I let the rectory and live in my own

house, so today Robert and I move to 29 Tredegar Square where 14 people lived in 1966 and 11 in 1971. It is a glorious Regency House with a 30ft drawing room on the first floor, and a slightly smaller dining room next to the kitchen on the ground floor. Four months ago I saw an article about it with a photo in *The Sunday Times* asking where is it? Kensington? Knightsbridge? It has five bedrooms but no study so I shall use the one in the church. Anywhere else in London it would have been out of our price range but Mile End is not fashionable and most of the houses in the Square are derelict.

20 November 1974. I have been trying to get the measure of the work to be done. In two tunnels of the crypt a weeknight club is held for Bangladeshi boys; they have a full-time worker paid by Social Services, so need little of my time. The other two crypt tunnels are used by about 70 homeless people four evenings a week and this is staffed by volunteers. George Appleton, later Archbishop of Jerusalem, started this in about 1960 when he was rector. Free food, washing facilities and clothing are provided, but most of all volunteers offer friendship. Helping give out clothing is a nightmare. At 7pm we throw open a stable door and men surge forward to the counter. Three men are allowed in at a time and I feel like an assistant in Harrods' menswear – 'This is too small.' 'This is too big.' 'How do you expect me to get into these trousers?' 'I don't like this colour.' I am assessing what needs to be done to make the centre more effective.

1 December 1974. Gerald is at St Botolph's for a confirmation, and comes to lunch afterwards with Robert and me. Before the meal he takes me into the dining room, sits me down and asks if I had been married. 'Bishop Robert burnt your file which was very irresponsible, tell me about yourself.' So I take a deep breath and tell him the full story. He looked apprehensive, but made no comment.

28 February 1975. Bearing in mind Bishop Robert's suggestion that a separate denomination for gays must be avoided at all

costs I write to +Gerald asking if Tom Bigelow, an Episcopalian priest from America, might use St Botolph's for a weekly bible study or service for the Fellowship of Christ the Liberator, a gay group which is the English branch of the Metropolitan Community Church. His bishop[25] has written to tell me saying that Tom is 'a fine priest'.

1 March 1975. 8.46am an underground train filled with rush-hour commuters overran the platform at Moorgate, smashed through the buffers and ploughed into a blind tunnel killing 29 people and injuring more than 70. It is the worst accident on the London tube system for 100 years. I sat in my study at Aldgate listening to ambulance sirens wondering what was going on. Fr Stanley Moore at St Botolph Bishopsgate was allowed into the tunnel and later told me he did not know what to do and felt he was in the way. A good exam question for ordinands – what should he have done? Chaplains in the war did not get in the way, but when not taking funerals or comforting the dying and listening to last messages they helped as orderlies in the hospitals or dressing stations.

10 March 1975. Representing St Botolph's, I am a committee member of *No Fixed Abode*, a coordinating organisation of East End agencies working with the homeless. Founded by Richard Smith, who has taught me so much in these first few months, it stops us duplicating work – although someone has unkindly said that if you see a homeless man in a hurry he has probably had breakfast with the Methodists, is on his way to lunch with the Anglicans, then supper with the RCs. He has a room in the Salvation Army. Isn't it impressive that Christians do most of the homeless work in East London? NFA asked me to do a publicity pamphlet which arrived today. Unfortunately the printer has made a mistake by swapping the answers to two questions:

Who are the helped?
Businessmen, housewives and students.

Who are the helpers?

Mainly middle-aged men who have a drink problem or a history of mental illness or violence.

21 March 1975. The Bishop interviews Tom Bigelow and decides he cannot give permission for the group to use St Botolph's. I should never have asked Gerald, but let the group use the church – I have learnt a lesson today.

22 March 1975. There are huge possibilities for St Botolph's and one is to develop the work with young people. I have always been impressed by David Randall, a curate in Poplar, who wants to be a detached youth worker in East London. He has a fiery temper and recently fell out with his vicar, Fr Bourne, tore his Licence up and stuffed it through Bishop Trevor Huddleston's letterbox. 'You shouldn't have done that, dearie,' said Trevor, and David now needs a job. So I asked Gerald to licence him at St Botolph's. Dennis Delderfield,[26] lay chairman of the Diocesan Synod, and two of his cronies get wind of it and try to stop it by telling him that the press know something detrimental about David. I gave the Bishop my word that the only thing that they might know is that David lives with a man, so Gerald called their bluff and appointed David. The heavens did not fall in.

15 June 1975. After preaching in Worcester Cathedral our host, Canon Eric Turnbull, took us to have tea with John Hencher, a former actor now a priest/teacher and John Cupper who works in an art gallery. They have been together seven years, live in a Herefordshire tea-cosy house near Kington and are great fun. When he was vicar of Amblecote a cheeky local reporter asked John H why he was not married, and he replied he wanted someone looking like Ingrid Bergman. The headline 'handsome vicar wants a wife' hit the local then the international papers and hundreds of letters poured in, one from a nun.

30 June 1975. Gerald summons me to London House and comes out of the General Synod to talk with me because he says

that Delderfield threatens to resign if David Randall isn't sacked. He is saying that two priests in Aldgate are practising gays, which is, of course, true. The Bishop, wise as always, suggests I meet Delderfield.

15 July 1975. I have a long chat with Dennis Delderfield who is not the bigoted ogre I expected, but a politician *manqué* and very right-wing. David shows him round the east end clubs which he visits regularly. In the end Dennis withdraws his objections providing David is supervised by three people including him.[27]

15 October 1975. Since my arrival in Aldgate I have been very concerned about our homeless centre in the crypt, which is staffed solely by volunteers and opens four evenings a week. I asked Eddy Stride, rector and in charge of Spitalfields Crypt, to loan me a worker but after three weeks I found him dead drunk outside the church so had to refer him to my old pal Dr Rodney Long.[28] Today Bishop Gerald has given me permission to employ Terry Drummond, a Church Army worker with experience in this field so I am mightily relieved.

1 January 1976. We begin to build up a team of full-time social workers to be with Terry. We now open five nights a week and they provide continuity. The youth club has closed because a new club has opened in Spitalfields, so *Kipper* a charity for teenagers who sleep rough (kip) in Tower Hamlets are using the two tunnels as a day centre. I am chairman and it was founded by Dan Jones, a large bearded man with a huge heart. He is a social worker and artist.

10 March 1976. Bishop Gerald who visited the crypt two nights ago writes, 'I am greatly impressed and proud of what you are doing.' After he had seen the homeless and their volunteers we took him to the Still and Star where Win Noonan, the publican, gave his visit to the clubs a flying start by giving him two double whiskies. Wearing a grey suit and tie and looking like a country squire, he was introduced by David as, 'My friend

Gerald.' 'How do you do?' booms that magnificent deep episcopal voice.

15 March 1976. I receive a letter from Mr Lindow the secretary saying I am elected to the Athenaeum – 'O, the Athenaeum where they understand all the arts and sciences except gastronomy and questions on any subject can be answered between 1 and 3pm'. My splendid predecessor at St Botolph's, Derek Harbord, 'one of Her Majesty's colonial judges retired' as the notice board outside the church used to proclaim, proposed me. When the committee said I was young (39) and asked if I had I written any books, Harbord replied, 'No, but he will.'

March 1976. Roger Royle has asked me to give the four Lyttelton Lectures at Eton, preach in the chapel and visit the boys during the day. Several months ago I asked Roger, who is Senior Conduct (chaplain), to assemble seven senior boys to help me do this and over several suppers we worked out a theme – PSEUD. What is real and what is not. The school has a confident effortless atmosphere (at £2,400 p.a. it comes at a price) but I am surprised that over 300 boys come each night to hear me. I get some of the group to heckle me or ask questions which causes a stir.

2 April 1976. I receive an urgent summons to see the Trollopian Archdeacon of London, Sam Woodhouse, so I hurry to Amen Court. Seated on a chintz-covered sofa sipping China tea I am told that the Bishop is anxious about the Gay Christian Movement's opening service in St Botolph's tomorrow, and would I explain. 'What is gay?' asks Sam, so I tell him. Later just before bedtime I received a call from Gerald just back from a City dinner saying he is angry and I must be at London House at 9.30am tomorrow. My heart sank.

3 April 1976. For ½ hour Gerald berates me for not asking him if an RC priest (Giles Hibbert) could preach, or if the service could or should be held. 'Why don't you keep quiet? I don't tell everyone what Mrs Ellison and I do in bed.' I try to explain the aims of the new organisation but carefully omit telling him they

will have an office in the tower. He says that regretfully he cannot stop the service as I am rector, nor can he forbid the inaugural meeting in the Cass school because I am chairman of governors. 'I want a copy of the sermon and a list of all the clergy present.' I arrive back at the church feeling worn out just as the meeting to discuss the draft constitution begins. I have a wedding at 3pm so the afternoon gathering is in the school hall but the Eucharist at 5pm is splendid and over 150 are in church. I don't tell anyone about the interview. I think that we have delayed too long in founding GCM. When 'Consenting Bill' passed through Parliament in 1967 other groups got going much more quickly. The first meeting of the Gay Liberation Front was in 1970 at the London School of Economics, and my first visit was soon afterwards when they had moved to All Saints Church Hall, Notting Hill.[29] Somewhat frustratingly I had to attend an initiation meeting in a side hall so I could be told the aims and objectives. Over the next few years GLF spawned Gay Switchboard, street theatre, Gays the Word bookshop, Ice Breakers, a counselling agency and an antipsychiatry group. We are a little late. It was not until last autumn that a few of us met in Southwark to get a Christian organisation going.

13 April 1976. In a letter received today replying to my report (which did not mention the clergy present) Gerald says that he 'thinks it unwise for homosexuals to group together as it draws criticism and hostility.' He warns me not to attract unnecessary attention to St Botolph's, and says that he was surprised and concerned to learn about the 3 April meeting. 'Your invitation was a breach of faith.' He wants to know why I had not mentioned it during his visit, and says he will consider moving David to another parish. 'I will not licence him yet.' Needless to say I am hurt by this, but I could not have asked permission for the GCM service because it would have been refused.

6 May 1976. For the last few months I have been planning a meeting of gay clergy (someone said that we would need to hire

the Albert Hall) but in fact 55 of us met today at the Royal Foundation of St Katharine in Limehouse. Peter Elers, Douglas Rhymes and I wrote to all our friends who would appreciate such a meeting, and phrased that it was for 'those who are homosexual or interested in the condition.' The cost was £1 for lunch and tea. Men came from as far away as Truro and Birmingham, and there were 10 hetero/bisexuals present. Douglas began with a paper on the theology of sexuality, and the day ended with a Eucharist at 5.30. Someone called it 'a welcome event' and we agreed to have two a year and I would, as secretary, issue invitations.

26 May 1976. I preside at Doreen Cordell's memorial service at St Botolph's. An amazing congregation fills the church because as well as her husband and family there are Girl Guides (she ran a troop) and many gay men who she counselled at the Albany Trust. Add to that a number of transvestites and transsexuals she helped over the years. I remember her telling me about a colonel in the Guards who at weekends became his sister in London. People would say, 'I'd like to meet your brother.' One of Doreen's specialities was to advise men-to-women transsexuals on make-up, dress etc. I shall miss her dreadfully, and shall never forget that she introduced Robert and me.

19 June 1976. A warm, friendly letter from Gerald about my interest in church history. I'm back in favour and in three years we have moved from 'Dear Johnson' to 'My dear Malcolm' and from 'My Lord' to 'My dear Bishop'.

1 December 1976. I wanted to have some input into the church working party who are preparing a report on homosexuality, so I sat down and wrote out the names of 100 clergy I know well who are predominantly or exclusively gay. Some are friends, some come to the consultation meetings and some have come to me for counselling over the last eight years in London. Eleven are 30 or under; 8 are monks or friars; 42 are parish priests; 22 in specialist ministries; 11 are in senior appointments – deans etc; 2 are retired and 15 have left the ministry – 4 to live with a partner.

It is interesting that 75 have no partner, 6 are gay but married and 19 have a gay partner (3 under 3 years). Of the 19 only 3 are in ordinary parishes where the vicarage is near the church, and 4 have left the ministry. The loneliness this must cause is worth pondering because it shows that at present it is almost impossible for a parish priest to live with a partner so he thus loses all the comfort and stability this brings. Forty-four of the 100 live in London which must help loneliness a little because of other gay clergy being near, and gay meeting places being more accessible.

So only 19 have partners but when I wrote down 100 hetero clergy I found 93 were married and 3 are separated from their wives.

Recently the Albany Trust did a survey of 2,082 gay men and found that 893 were in a relationship of more than 6 months and 574 were living with the partner. This is a significantly larger percentage than the clergy.

21 December 1976. Robert and I take my godchildren Ann and Nicola, aged 13, to see Nureyev dance in *The Nutcracker* at Covent Garden, and their mothers meet us afterwards in the Waldorf Hotel in Aldwych. When they got home the girls talked mainly not about Nureyev but about the free peanuts and crisps in the hotel.

22 December 1976. I invite all the gay organisations to send representatives to a special Carol Service in St Botolph's and most respond. I was worried about publicity – 'Queers sing in City church' – but there was none at all, and the heavens did not fall in. I decided not to have the carol *Deck the Hall* with its lines 'Troll we now the Christmas message' and 'Don we now our gay apparel'.

24 December 1976. For the Crisis at Christmas Midnight Service Sister Pauline, an RC nun, has objected to a concelebrated Eucharist taking place – as last year – so in St Mary's redundant church Lambeth we have to have separate services. I am very angry about this. Nine hundred meals are served and about 100

come to the service.

7 January 1977. I visit King's College Cambridge chapel to see the Rubens *Adoration of the Magi*, painted in 1634, which is now placed behind the altar. It really doesn't fit there, but where else could it be? It gave me so much inspiration when it hung on the main staircase of Eaton Hall when I was doing my officer training there in March 1956. We had no idea it was a Rubens, and it is a miracle it was not damaged by our boisterous water and cream fights. In 1959 Major AE Allnatt bought it from the estate of the Duke of Westminster for a record £275,000, and gave it to King's in November 1961.

8 January 1977. I show the members of the London Appreciation Society around the church, crypt and school. They were particularly interested in seeing where Jack the Ripper killed Catherine Eddowes on 30 September 1888 and hearing that her throat had been cut and her intestines placed over her right shoulder. The playground gates now cover the site.

12 January 1977. I gave two seminars on the gay issue at Cuddesdon, my old theological college. I have done this several times but on this occasion the atmosphere is electric as four students have complained to the governors about a member of staff making a pass at a student. I always talk openly about my own sexuality and after Compline I heard an older, ex-Army student saying, 'My room is next to Malcolm's, will I be safe?'

9 February 1977. What is to be done with the three reredos panels behind the altar at St Botolph's? They were destroyed in the disastrous 1965 fire[30] and are covered by red curtains. Today Patrick Reyntiens in a combat jacket accompanied by a dog came to see them. He thinks that they should be wood veneered and will ask John Piper what he thinks.

16 February 1977. The splendidly named Sir Hugh Munro-Lucas-Tooth,[31] who was Under Secretary of State at the Home Department 1952–55 in Churchill's government, is chair of governors of the Raine's Foundation School in Stepney, and

although I have been a governor for six years he always keeps me in my place by whispering loudly to the Clerk whenever I want to speak, 'What's his name?' He looks and sounds like Harold Macmillan and dislikes me because I have always opposed his plan to move Raines, the best school in the East End, out to Essex following the example of Davenant, Parmiters etc. This is disgraceful as these schools were founded and funded for Stepney children, and they should remain. Fortunately Raines has very little money and the site would not raise enough cash to buy land in Essex.

3 March 1977. The diocese is allowing me to rent for £7.25 per week the top floor flat of the former Whitechapel rectory. It will make a good home for David Randall and he tells me that he has found all sorts of 1920s Russian banknotes hidden in the attic which suggests that the Russian émigrés lived here. The most recent occupant was the formidable Michael Hodgins who retired as Archdeacon of Hackney and Secretary of the London Diocesan Fund three years ago. He wasn't agile enough to climb into the attic but he was a wily old bird, severe and formidable and has taught me how to be a chairman because he is still chair of the Cass Foundation.[32] He is one of nature's bachelors and with his cigarette holder looks a bit like Noel Coward.

12–14 May 1977. The Sir John Cass's Foundation, of which I am an ex-officio governor, has bought for £65,000 a huge house in Wales near Machynlleth for the children of our two schools to visit. Today a party of governors go by train and bus to visit it and we stay in splendid local hotel. John Roberts, the very talented warden, shows us round and tells us that often the teenagers on arrival change into the special outdoor clothes then jump in the stream and cover themselves with mud. Most of them have never been in the country before or seen the sea. This visit is a good opportunity for us Cass governors to get to know each other, but there is no jumping in streams. Mrs Robinson, an elderly flighty City lady who lives in the Inns of Court, spends most of her time ogling the chairman.

1 June 1977. Eagle Star has moved into the new office block next to the church, and I called on the office manager Tom Alder recently and suggested that some of the staff might like 'tea with the vicar'. Today the last party was held, and about 200 have come into St Botolph's, had tea and looked round the church and crypt. I greatly enjoy our links with the local firms, and must try and set up a Business Houses Council similar to the one at All Hallows-by-the-Tower.

7 June 1977. Silver Jubilee Day. Mother, now 66, and I arrive at St Paul's Cathedral at 7.30am and stand for over 5 hours without moving. We must be mad. Lots going on – dustmen and Heath were cheered, Callaghan booed. Commonwealth Prime Ministers arrive in a fleet of cars (and left later in a bus), and assorted bishops and other notorious evil livers enter by the south door. At 10.30 a band started to play and then the Speaker's pantomime coach creaks up Ludgate Hill. The royals arrive in open landaus then HM and the Duke trundle past at 11.30 in the vulgar, gilded State Coach which was used for the Coronation. St Paul's doors were then shut and we were left outside twiddling our thumbs. What a lost opportunity to broadcast the service to us plebs outside. The crowd was huge by this time, and the Queen and Duke emerged at 12.30 for their walkabout to Guildhall. We went home to Tredegar Square for lunch, and in the afternoon Father disappeared for over two hours then returned to say he had been at a street party. Above a table groaning with beer and goodies was a notice 'OAPs help yourself' so he did.

10 June 1977. A few weeks ago Philip Corby, the Master of St Botolph's Tower, came rushing into the church kitchen – 'Would you like a hostel?' Apparently he is on the Board of the World of Property Housing Trust[33] who have purchased a long lease on the Cass estate in Hackney, and at a meeting Prince Philip their Patron had asked them what they are doing for the homeless of the East End. Nothing is the reply. Today at the WPHT meeting I

was told that they will buy the derelict land at 257 Victoria Park Road costing £11,000 for our hostel. This is great news. The hostel can be furnished for around £7,000 so I must start fund-raising; I do not want second-hand stuff.

8 June 1977. A seated statue of the Virgin Mary was brought back from Walsingham earlier this year by the parish pilgrims led by David Randall. Half the congregation hated it and half loved it – Monica Rejman, a tiny dumpy Polish lady who lives at the local Salvation Army hostel and always comes to church in national costume with lace cap, decided she would 'knit Mother some dresses.' Trudie Eulenburg, our parish worker, calls the statue 'ze doll on ze shelf,' because as I didn't know where to put it I placed it on a window sill. Today one of our crypt men threw it on to the floor breaking it into smithereens. Half cheered, half cried.

15 June 1977. A Garden Party at the Athenaeum, and Robert and I were at the back of a long queue when Archbishop Athenagoras of Thyateira arrived in full gear with silver-topped ebony cane. He gazed at handsome Robert and without looking at me said, 'Father, introduce your friend,' which I did, and he then said, 'Archbishops go to the front of the queue' and swept Robert away leaving me with an elderly white-suited Greek shipping millionaire. Not a bad exchange, I suppose.

20 June 1977. The second Consultation for gay clergy and we had a 'fares pool' to help those travelling a long distance. Perhaps the most moving part of the day is the Eucharist when we stand in a circle round the altar.

26 June 1977. As it is Gay Pride Week we hold a Service of Liberation for the gay community at 3pm, and representatives of Christian gay groups turn up – Quest (RC), GCM, Quakers, MCC. Even the Jewish Gay Group turn up.

29 June 1977. I took Joy Drewett Browne, the secretary of the Royal Foundation of St Katharine, to watch Chris Evert vs. Virginia Wade on the Centre Court at Wimbledon. Joy was

playing truant as there is a governors meeting there today. 'But it doesn't matter,' she said, as the Bishop of London can't come, he has an important engagement. When we looked at the Royal Box there was Gerald Ellison.

31 July 1977. My tea parties with Eagle Star have paid off because today one of the underwriters on the fifth floor telephoned to ask if I knew someone was rolling lead up on the church roof. I called the City police who came at once, and the man having climbed down was asked what he was doing. 'I was having a rest.' 'Arrest is what I am here for,' said the copper.

3 August 1977. Mr Bloch of Barter Street is a Dickensian old gent who sits in the corner of his cluttered second-hand book/print shop. His aged assistant hisses at customers, 'Don't buy anything, his prices are high.' In fact they are very low, and I have bought Spy and Ape prints for £3 and under. These are caricatures of famous people and were in *Vanity Fair* each week from January 1869 until February 1914, and the write-up with them was always perceptive and amusing. I am collecting the clergy although there are 104 and some are not very interesting. The judges in their scarlet are the most sought after. Mr Bloch has stacks of brown files on and under a central table, and you can find amazing things such as signed photos of Queen Victoria.

11 August 1977. A charming, gentle John Piper comes at my invitation to look at the three bare reredos panels behind the altar and make suggestions. He thinks that we should ignore the Rubens stained glass window above as the eye cannot contain both. He asks what I want and I say a 'Gate of Heaven' theme because we are a gate church and the altar is where heaven and earth meet during the communion, so is thus an entrance or gateway to the next world. The side panels might contain angels to guard the gate. He sits in the pews and meditates on this but looks a bit confused. 'What does the Gate of Heaven look like?' he asks me. 'No idea,' and we both roar with laughter.

15 August 1977. A member of the City Corporation tells me

that Basil Watson, the redneck rector of St Lawrence Jewry who boasts that he wears a dinner jacket more than a cassock, was heard at Mansion House saying that St Botolph's is 'full of queers.' At a meeting of Sion College Court he once told me not to be insolent. I had asked him as chairman why more money was spent on entertaining than buying or repairing books.

14 September 1977. 'Ho ho,' said Gerald Ellison, 'you are in for a lot of pain.' I had told him that I was to be admitted to the London Hospital in Whitechapel for a piles operation. The last operation I had was to remove my tonsils in 1946 with chloroform. When I came round then the nurse was cleaning the instruments in a big silver container by my bedside. I came out of the London Hospital yesterday after 2 weeks, and it certainly was painful although it had its brighter side. I was in a large open ward next to a street trader Matt, whose family filled the ward at visiting time. We got on very well and on my last morning I woke up to hear sniggering, and when I opened my eyes he had put flowers around me with a notice above my head: 'Malcolm Johnson, priest and martyr'. I warmed to him because at supper one evening a know-all patient, who turned out to be a psychiatrist from Hampstead, was saying that all homosexuals are perverted and dangerous to children. Matt said to him, 'You obviously don't know any; that is a load of crap.'

I had hundreds of visitors mainly East End clergy so everyone in the ward thought that I was dying because they all prayed over me. Norry McCurry, the vicar of Stepney, arrived at 9pm one evening and was distressed that I was upset because I had not been to the lavatory for several days; I was afraid of the pain. He went home and arrived just before midnight with a tin of prunes, and made me eat them. At 5am there was a gigantic explosion and I didn't make it to the lavatory, and fell in my mess. A sweet nurse picked me up, put me on the seat and then washed me later. The pain made sleeping difficult and the next night in the darkness I got out of bed and buried my head in the blanket, then someone put their arms around me and cuddled me and gave me painkillers. The power of touch; the laying on of hands. I never saw that tough-looking charge nurse again; I would like to have thanked him. A formal letter arrived amongst the cards, 'The Aldgate Church Cass Society sends you their wishes for a speedy recovery. Voting was 5 for and 4 against'. When I got home I found a urine bottle had been put in my luggage probably by Matt.

20 September 1977. I went to Phillips sale room for the lead soldier sale, and because the Douglas Fairbanks collection was being sold we had TV cameras and lights. I have collected these since 1947 when they were made again after the war by Britains Ltd, and I now have a private army, as the insurance company describes it, of over 1,000. Many of Fairbanks were B or C grade, but I did buy an A set of 12 State Trumpeters of the Household Cavalry for £65. When I was in my early teens they gave me a world of fantasy to live in; and during school holidays because I had few friends, I would take over one of the rooms and for a week put on a huge parade; never a battle as that would damage them. My 1953 Coronation involved 800 pieces and the State Coach. I sincerely regret that when I was 17, I took notice of my mother's taunt, 'You are too old to play with soldiers,' and gave up collecting.

23 September 1977. John Piper has produced a model of his idea for the centre panel behind the altar based, at the suggestion of Benjamin Britten who he visited just before he died in December last year, on the 18th century *Glory* behind the altar of Framlingham church. At the centre is a ball of golden fire with ceramic rays reaching out to the dark clouds at the edge of the canvas. I like the *Glory* idea but sadly the PCC say it looks like a dartboard, so it is not acceptable. How do I tell him?

11 October 1977. Holidaying in Malta Robert and I go most nights to the Lantern in Valletta – the only gay bar on the island. Tonight three men caught our eye and came over offering us a

drink. They turned out to be a monsignor ('call me Revd Mother') and two other RC priests. They said we were known as Tablecloth and Prince Charles because of Robert's shirt and my likeness to Charles. At midnight they said that they had a present for us, and soon afterwards two very handsome young waiters from the Birdcage Cafe in Medina joined us.

22 October 1977. A big shock as despite all my demands two girls turn up for a Service of Blessing, one wearing a suit and one a bridal gown attended by five bridesmaids. Their parents were also present. I rushed through the service which was just as well as a *News of the World* reporter arrived soon after they left asking if a wedding had taken place. Quite truthfully I said no and closed the door. I have about three of these services each month, so will make sure this never happens again. One day perhaps it won't matter if some, probably only a few, gays and lesbians want to ape heterosexual marriage.

24 October 1977. Norman Pittenger speaks to the Consultation and stays the night with Robert and I. We take it in turns to listen to him as he never stops talking – but always interestingly. He is now 72 and is retired from the General Theological seminary New York. Eleven years ago he went to live in Rome with Carlo, but then settled in Cambridge where he became a senior member of King's College. His book *Time for Consent* (1969) asks for the Church to accept gays and caused a furore at the time. The *Church Times*[34] refused to review it, and Heffers the bookshop in Cambridge wouldn't put it in the window. It sold 10,000 copies and was just one of his 90 books – usually on process theology and AN Whitehead. One is dedicated to Robert and me. Norman says he is the Barbara Cartland of theology.

26 October 1977. Michael Bourne, a priest member of the Advisory Council, suggests we have a hanging pyx above the altar in the shape of a dove to contain the Sacrament. Splendid idea.

27 October 1977. *Men Only's* editor Roger Baker gave a talk in church on 'Pornography'. I decided that we had heard too much from Mrs Whitehouse[35] and another view should be put. He told the audience of around 80 that one man's porn is another man's pin-up. It should not be on public display, but available. He found meat in a butcher's window offensive so realised one had to be careful about people's feelings. I asked Mrs Whitehouse to speak to students at Queen Mary College five years ago and hundreds turned up. Antony Grey[36] looking at this lady remarked that 'the sin of the English is not buggery but humbuggery.'

11 November 1977. David Randall has moved to be vicar of St Clement Notting Dale and I feel proud of the work he has done at St Botolph's particularly in the Kipper Project for homeless teenagers.

21 December 1977. An odd evening. Ten of St Botolph's congregation go to Petticoat Square to join 20 assorted elderly Jewish residents to sing carols (yes, carols). Afterwards we go to their club for bingo and more carols and refreshments including pork sausages.

7–20 January 1978. Another cruise. This time I fly to Tangier, embark, sail along the North African coast to Malta, entering Grand Harbour at Valletta. No bad weather fortunately, and Captain Dubois tells me that, 'A Captain of calm waters,' is someone who cannot cope with trouble according to Nicholas Montsarrat. After Piraeus we get to Haifa where we have a ridiculously short visit to the Holy Land. Highlights for me were sitting quietly meditating on the Mount of Olives with very few people around, seeing the Shepherds' Supermarket at Bethlehem, and walking down the Via Dolorosa when I heard one of our schoolboys say to his friend:

'You know, it makes you think.'
'What does it make you think?'

'Dunno, but it makes you think.'

I was very preoccupied because Ben my spaniel is having a very serious operation today and might die, so I was rather tearful. However, Robert called the ship when we returned to say all is well. We visited Bodrum then flew home from Malta. These cruises are a marvellous free holiday with five-star food and a cabin all to myself.

8 February 1978. I am a trustee of Upton House which is the old people's home next door to us in Tredegar Square. It was founded by Fr Groser after the last war but is now in a sad state of repair. At the trustees meeting a week ago Jack Wolkind, the genial old Chief Executive of Tower Hamlets, suggested that we give it to the Council. He phoned today to say that it is not ours to give because Barnardo's own the freehold, but had forgotten about it. So when we have rehoused the old people we will return it to them.

11 February 1978. Since 1969 I have taken Services of Blessing for gay couples providing I see them twice beforehand, there are only 12 people present and they do not say where the ceremony is held. Couples come from all over the place, and today two young men, John and Brian, came from Dagenham for their service. They invited Robert and I to a sumptuous reception afterwards where all the other guests seemed to be tough working-class bisexual married men working at Ford's. Some of them knew the Krays; some go to Bethnal Green baths for fun.

16 March 1978. Am hugely relieved that the op which my spaniel had was completely successful. Poor old Ben kept making stones in his bladder which piled up as he couldn't pass them through the penis. After removing them surgically they started to form again, so the vet suggested re-routing the urethra through the anus and that is what was done. Now Ben pees through the rear end, so any dog that comes up for a sniff gets drenched.

17 March 1978. Gay Christians suffer greatly from members of the hierarchy who are frightened of their own homosexual feelings so hit out at openly gay people. I am trying to appoint a priest-counsellor and a very suitable candidate, George Bright, who is training to be an analyst, was interviewed today by Bishop Mark Hodson. He vetoes him because he lives with someone. My friends have always told me that the Bishop is probably gay, and only married late in life. Hypocrisy makes me throw up.

18 March 1978. I wrote to +Gerald about today's GCM service and how the Movement is now a very responsible one, and he replied, 'My main irritation is their taking the word gay and giving it a new meaning. It makes it very difficult to use the word in common parlance.' If that is all he is worried about...

20 April 1978. Jim Martin, former distinguished Methodist minister at the East End Bow Mission, has died. I shall never forget him coming to see me five years ago to 'confess' his wrong-headedness over the gay issue and the derogatory remarks he had made over the years. His gay son had taught him to rethink his views.

18 May 1978. I go to St John's Wood to the flat of John Phillips (formerly Vassall) for a drink and chat. He comes to the SK Group, is a devout RC and now doing an administrative job at Charterhouse. In October 1962 aged 38 he was sentenced to 18 years imprisonment because he had pleaded guilty to giving secrets to the Russians for cash. He was a clerical officer in Moscow and the KGB blackmailed him because of his homosexuality, so he started spying for them by photographing Admiralty documents after he returned to London in 1956. He was released in 1972, and I like him although he is rather fussy and prissy. He comes to some of our parties at Tredegar Square, but has no partner.

2 June 1978. An irate Sir Bernard Waley-Cohen, our alderman, phones to tell me off for having a speaker in 'our Ward church' from the League Against Cruel Sports. 'They damage property,'

he says. How about the damage his hounds inflict on stags on Dartmoor (he is Master). I suggest that he provides a speaker from his viewpoint, but make it clear I will oppose his views. I have never heard kindly old Bernard so agitated.

12 June 1978. I am going to appoint John Lee, once a research scientist in Australia and now at St Teilo Portmead, as a priest/counsellor. Sadly his marriage has collapsed. My church-warden Billy Dove at the PCC says we need 'ordinary normal staff.' I got angry and said we don't have ordinary normal wardens, which didn't go down too well. The Bishop suggests we employ John as a social worker not a priest because he cannot licence him, so that is what I shall do.

14 June 1978. I was expecting opposition to my suggestions for a statue of Mary. Connie Cook, a sculptress in Much Hadham, has produced a design of a young Jewish girl holding a crown of thorns. It will stand on a shelf on the base of which is the inscription 'A sword will pierce your heart too'. Mary looks through the thorns towards the crypt where we see so much suffering. Everyone likes it, but the churchwarden hopes that it will not be lifted up, carried about or covered with flowers.

21 June 1978. One of the most unpleasant evenings of my life because I went to a meeting of the South Hackney Residents' Association to tell them about the projected hostel in Victoria Park Road for 22 homeless men. Mrs Fowkes, the chairperson, and her friends shrieked at me non-stop like fishwives, saying that I was building on common land and the hostel residents would attack or seduce their children and molest old ladies. The building, they said, was three floors so too high, too near the shops and the rooms are too small. The 100 people present were hysterical and refused to listen to my explanation that the land was a derelict bombsite which had had houses on it before the war, and that our staff would be carefully chosen to supervise and care for the residents. A lot of the anger stemmed from the fact that their houses are owned by the Cass/WPHT estate. One

of the women said, 'At last we see a Cass governor face to face.' I went home shattered, had three large gins then went to bed.

1 July 1978. The South Hackney Residents' Association is mailing all the local houses to ask them to object to the hostel, so I decide to mail 500 households with a pamphlet 'The Facts'.

9 July 1978. I have got to know many of the staff at Sedgwick Forbes and I recently suggested to the chairman that he ask Donald Coggan to lunch to tell him about reinsurance as they are the largest reinsurance firm in the City. Today the directors entertained him and I was invited. After each course we moved places so that everyone could chat to the Archbishop. He has a great gift of talking simply and directly to you in that magnificent voice and making you feel at home. I have been a fan of his since Durham days when as Bishop of Bradford he gave us excellent lectures on preaching. I value our links with Sedgwick's not just because of the cash they give us for the crypt and their splendid Carol Service, but because George Foster the receptionist collects used clothing for us. He saw my notice outside the church, 'Take off your clothes', and we are given some very smart suits. Michael Riesco, a director of Sedgwick's, and Molly his wife tour Petworth where they live and bring in all sorts of smart gear. The firm has a magnificent John Piper tapestry *The Gates of the City of London* hanging in their entrance hall.[37] Peter de Rougemont, one of the directors, knows him.

18 July 1978. I am on holiday in Boston, Massachusetts and I went to the St Botolph Club for lunch. It's like the Athenaeum and I sat next to an elderly toad-like gentleman who was being supplied with endless martinis. 'Who are you?' he asked. 'I'm an Episcopalian priest.' 'I hate the Episcopal Church.' It transpired he was the owner of the largest skyscraper in town, the Hancock Tower. Whilst it was being built the nearby Copley Plaza Hotel and Holy Trinity Church began to keel over. He bought the hotel, but was being sued for millions of dollars by Holy Trinity Vestry.

23 July 1978. I have to preach in a Universalist Unitarian

church so ask a friend who is of that persuasion what they believe. 'Not a lot, just don't talk too much about Jesus.'

1 September 1978. John Lee begins work as a member of our team which will take some of the counselling work off me, but for the time being Gerald will not license him. Fit as a flea, he is a real charmer and a trained group analyst. He is now married to Sue who we all love.

7 September 1978. Early this morning my father, aged 68, died suddenly of a brain haemorrhage. Robert and I drive to Great Yarmouth and find Mother dazed and sad. They had not had a very close marriage, but she hates to be on her own, and will find life very difficult indeed.

9 September 1978. I go with Mother to pay our respects to Papa in his coffin and for the first time I see that he has mousy brown hair – always he had Brylcreemed it black. To say goodbye I kiss him on the forehead, the first time I have ever kissed him, although Robert once kissed him goodnight at our house after kissing Mother. He didn't seem too bothered.

11 September 1978. Father's funeral at St Nicholas Great Yarmouth. As we prepare to go in I tell Mother to take deep breaths which was Father's cure for feeling nervous. The undertakers take him in on a trolley, lazy bastards. Why can't they carry him? The large congregation includes the Mayor, friends and lots of women who worked for him in the family clothing firm which was sold recently because his son had gone off to be a priest. Their letters have reduced us all to tears. The machinists wrote:

His life was full of kindly deeds, a helping hand to all our needs.
A cheerful smile, a heart of gold, the nicest boss the world could hold.

My father was a gentle, kind, macho man. He rarely swore and would not hurt a fly. In his younger days he had a fierce temper, and I would lay awake at night hearing him and Mother rowing, vowing not to go to sleep until they stopped. He had a nice sense of humour and always called me 'old boy'. His mother drank herself to death when he was 11, and Frank his father, 'the governor', would not allow him or his brother to go to boarding school or university. 'I want my boys at home,' which was strange as they had to have their meals with the housekeeper in the kitchen. Grandfather married again when father was 19 and he loathed Mabel the snobbish stepmother, as I did. Soon after her marriage she was showing some ladies round the large house in Norfolk Square, and threw open the door to her bedroom – 'This is my boudoir' – to find that Father had put gin bottles on all the tables. During the war they lived in Acle near us but we never saw them.

2 October 1978. George Meldrum, a camp Godfrey Winnish man who comes to church, asked me to take his mother's funeral, so I go to visit their house in Forest Gate where I find mother laid out in an open coffin in the front room. George says he sleeps by her side, and asks me if he might record my prayers so I launch forth with the last rites and commendation prayers, finishing with a flourish. 'Oh dear,' says George. 'I forgot to switch it on, would you say it again?' So I do.

5 October 1978. I have founded a new charity 'The Lodge Project' to set up our hostel – this enables us to get donations from secular Trusts. I am now also on the Board of WPHT, and an elderly member, Hilda Bazalgette, will be my deputy chairman. A Girton girl, she is formidable and would disapprove of 'chair'. A widow of long standing, she has a great affection for the East End, and her smart, sumptuous hats mean we call her Dame Hilda. She arrives in a hired car driven by 'Jones'.

15 October 1978. A letter has arrived from the Maritime Trust asking if I would like to travel on board the *Lydia Eva* from Great Yarmouth to St Katharine's dock where it will be part of the historic ships collection.[38] One of the last steam drifters to be

built (1930), it was named after my grandmother Johnson's sister. They were daughters of Harry Eastwick who built and owned drifters/trawlers in the days when 500 vessels fished for herring from Yarmouth. In October 1937 she landed 221 crans – a cran is around 1,000 herring. My grandmother, Annie, died in 1921 aged only 37 when my father was 11. Dear Father was not sentimental and all he kept of hers was a large ostrich feather fan. A year ago I asked where it was to be told, 'I've given it to the Amateur Dramatic Society.' I won't travel to London on the boat as there is so much going on at present.

23 October 1978. Fifth gay clergy Consultation and 60% of the 50 men present come from outside London so it shows that there is a need for this gathering. One hundred ninety-four were invited and 37 sent apologies.

24 October 1978. Whilst at home my mother asked what will happen to our family money when she and I have died. I suggest Robert will have it. 'Is it fair that a stranger will have it?' Robert and I have been together for nine years and she has stayed often with us so this is extremely hurtful to me.

1 November 1978. I am still doing counselling work and see around 10 people each week. Today a dreary 35 year old man drones on and on, and I begin to feel dozy when he suddenly says, 'The last priest I saw went to sleep. I had to wait until he woke up, then I asked him why he had done it and he said I was very boring. Do you think I'm boring?' My three-year counselling training jumps to my aid, and I asked him, 'Do *you* think that you are boring?'

15 November 1978. As the Gay Christian Movement is in our tower I sit in on the interviews to appoint a part-time administrative secretary to replace Fiona. Richard Kirker is the obvious choice. Handsome, young and intelligent, Runcie made him a deacon but declined to priest him.

8 December 1978. Lunch at the Athenaeum with my St Botolph's predecessor Derek Harbord who is responsible for my

being elected a member two years ago. He was one of Her Majesty's colonial judges and had a train all to himself in Ghana so that he could travel around hanging people. Now 76 he is the most delightful, witty person and calls me *the tightrope walker*. When GCM arrived in St Botolph's he wrote me a boring press handout to put reporters off the scent. In *Who's Who* he lists his interests as grandchildren and reading ecclesiastical whodunits. He has a clipped, squeaky voice and can be terrifying, but we get on famously. He was ordained a priest then trained as a barrister, became an RC and went out to Africa. On retirement he came home, reverted to Anglicanism, and when he was 60 his old pal Bishop Robert Stopford offered him St Botolph's where he stayed until he was 72.

16 December 1978. John Lee tells me he is enjoying his counselling work but occasionally gets chased around his study by men who are expecting more. I told him he was fortunate because it has never happened to me. Sue, his wife, must wonder what sort of set-up they have landed in. Several senior churchmen are seeing him for counselling, and I told him to say to his admirers, 'Thank you but no thank you.'

Sunday 17 December 1978. Carol Service for the gay community and around 250 come, overflowing into the gallery. I always ask representatives of various organisations to read, sing (there is also a quartet) etc, and tonight the heavy leather men took the collection with very good results. Mince pies and mulled wine afterwards.

1 January 1979. We usually now spend the turn of the year with the Two Johns in Herefordshire who are perfect hosts and treat us to wonderful food and introduce us to interesting people like the author Peter Parker. Visits to Hay-on-Wye bookshops are a bonus. Today I walked alone up Hergest Ridge and was so happy I sang the *Te Deum* much to other walkers' surprise.

19 January 1979. Apparently my entry in the Gay Switchboard files says, 'Best priest in London, good with girls.'

12 February 1979. I have invited the chairmen of the large firms to join me and Sir Bernard for lunch in the boardroom of our school next to the church, and six come and five send a director. The room makes a grand setting because it has 33 painted seventeenth century panels which were removed from a house in Billingsgate when the present school was built in 1906. The figures on the panels are hilarious: sea monsters, Indians, two tiny black men having a smoke, and big white women ordering little men around.[39] After lunch I explain my idea of a Business Houses Council consisting of a representative from each firm. We would meet bi-monthly to plan talks in the church and special events such as Carol Services. They all seem very keen, and a date is fixed for another lunch (at Sedgwick's) to begin it all.

21 March 1979. I visit Yarmouth to see my mother now 68 and getting over Father's death mainly because a toy boy of 56, Bert Prior, is living with her, and doing everything for her. A fortnight after the funeral he appeared at the door with an orchid and said, 'I have always admired you; if I can do anything for you let me know.' A fortnight later another orchid, and a month later another one, so she invited him in and he has remained. I cannot stand him but have to pretend that I think he is great – for her sake. Obviously I am grateful for him being in the house particularly because recently Mother saw someone climbing over the back wall into the garden, and had to call the police. He cooks, cleans, drives and does the garden. She says she won't marry him, so at clerical gatherings when oldies complain about young people today living in sin I can say, 'Like my mother.'

2 April 1979. I get a distress call from one of my 13 godchildren – a boy of 12 who is at a prep school in Kent, so I dash down and take him out for a tea of egg, beans, chips, sausage etc. I ask him if he is upset because his parents are divorcing. 'Oh no, I have always known that they would. The trouble is my dad is gay, shall I tell him I know?' I suggest that is

not a good idea although it is true. His father has not yet admitted it to himself.

4 May 1979. Petticoat Lane is in St Botolph's parish, and although the residents are nearly all Jewish there is one German family, the three Ebert sisters whose parents arrived here before the First World War. Today I took the funeral of the remaining sister who a fortnight ago sent for me from the London Hospital in Whitechapel. She thrust a package into my hands and said, 'This is for the donkeys and the Church.' I said prayers with her and when I got home there was £3,000 in notes. She died soon afterwards, and I phoned the Donkey Sanctuary which I know in Devon to tell them the news.

6 June 1979. Freddy Kobler, multimillionaire former chairman of Grand Metropolitan, comes to dinner with his wealthy Maltese boyfriend Anton. Robert cooks a superb meal as we are hoping that Freddy might help with a grant for St Botolph's work among the gay community. We also invite two very handsome men – Greg Richards, an Australian prison chaplain in Essex and his hunk of a boyfriend Leigh Bartlett from South Africa.

17 June 1979. Robert and I give a dinner for 12 friends to mark our 10th anniversary, and the guest of honour is Fr Fabian Cowper who is partly to blame for us meeting. When Robert was a 20 year old undergraduate at the City University, Fabian, who was the Catholic chaplain, gave a talk on homosexuality on behalf of the Albany Trust. The next day Robert rang Doreen Cordell the Trust's social worker who saw him. When she discovered that he was an Anglican she said he must be referred to Fr Johnson not Fr Cowper – much to Robert's disappointment as he thought Fabian was very dishy. He proposed our health tonight and described us as 'great hosts at all times.'

1 July 1979. Two hundred people attend the Gay Pride Service in St Botolph's with an orchestra of 15 conducted by Andrew Charity. To make up the number Andrew had invited some rather right-wing players, and afterwards apologised to them. They

thought that he was apologising for it being a religious event, and were certainly not bothered by a gay congregation.

6 July 1979. Sometimes I think that my heart will break, sometimes I feel clamped by a terrible feeling of helplessness; there is no way out of bereavement. Ben our cocker spaniel had to be put to sleep today – I held him in my arms whilst the vet did it. For 16 years he has been my constant companion and at one time was the only reason why I didn't end my life. Both Robert and I are devastated and Nancy, our daily, sat on the back doorstep and howled. Few would understand our grief. Amazing how these little creatures wind their way around your heart.

2 August 1979. I went to St Joseph's Hospice in Hackney to say goodbye to Brother Adrian, the Franciscan who was my spiritual director for several years. I thanked him for encouraging me to take so many retreats, but he said it was he who should thank me. I felt so very sad as I left.

3 August 1979. Brother Simeon phones to tell me Brother Adrian has died with five handsome brothers at his bedside which must have pleased him. He was one of the few Franciscans who take their vow of celibacy seriously, and he has taught me so much about taking retreats, which is useful because I usually take one or two each year.

12 August 1979. Yesterday Robert and I went to lunch with Freddy Kobler at his mansion near East Grinstead with huge grounds and sculptures by Elisabeth Frink. A splendid meal and just as we were leaving he said, 'I want to give you something,' so my heart leapt – I desperately need funding for a counsellor. He handed me a pot with a tiny ivy plant. When I got home I planted it, but unfortunately Robert mowed the lawn this afternoon and cut its head off.[40]

20 August 1979. We have been given planning permission to build the hostel for 22 men in Victoria Park Road despite the campaign of the South Hackney Residents' Association. Laus

Deo. I am thrilled, and will now form a steering committee and start raising money.

7 September 1979. Robert Runcie, the newly appointed (not elected) Archbishop of Canterbury, promises to throw away the platitude machine. He always has an amusing story to tell – when he went to St Albans the local paper wrote about his Enthornment.

6 October 1979. I speak at a weekend conference of mainly elderly ladies at the Royal Foundation of St Katharine on 'Escape from the shadows' in a series on relationships – marriage, celibacy, gay etc. A surprisingly good selection of questions including one from an old lady of about 85 who asked, 'What exactly do gay men do together?' It is the same question Jim Thompson asked me last year when he became Bishop of Stepney. I sat him down and told him everything. Well, perhaps not everything.

19 October 1979. A Report on homosexuality is published today.[41] Three of the members of the commission who wrote it are gay including the Revd Michael Day, but they have obviously had no influence on their confreres. The Report is an insult as it says that gay loving is 'morally and socially' not equivalent to heterosexual marriage. So we are second class and will behave accordingly. It says that gay clergy if they are open about their sexuality should resign. There is no mention whatsoever of civil rights, and the *Daily Telegraph* somewhat surprisingly says that young people will ignore it.

25 October 1979. I wrote to tell Michael Day that I am surprised he signed the report, and he replied that my membership of the Athenaeum had made me pompous.

29 October 1979. I receive a six-page handwritten letter from +Gerald. I had written to him attacking the insulting Gloucester Report. He considers that my views are so far removed from the standards of Christian teaching that they are unacceptable to the majority of Christian people. 'Homosexuals must be celibate. I

cannot believe our generation has been vouchsafed some under-standing of the issues denied to our forefathers or that we have any right to cast aside the traditional teaching of the Church.'

5–9 November 1979. I am on retreat at the Franciscan house in Cerne Abbas Dorset where I used to stay regularly until recently. In my meditations and walks I realise that the certainty of my beliefs has evaporated. Everything is now tentative and although I work for the management, as John Betjeman calls God, I rarely feel his presence. I have become cynical about the Church and feel an outsider. I ponder how I spend my work time, and estimate that a quarter of it is on counselling and care of gays; another quarter on the educational work of schools; 10% on homeless work and hostel plans; 10% on staff care; and the rest on worship, admin, preaching etc. I am now chair of governors of both Cass schools and enjoy it.

12 November 1979. The seventh Consultation for gay clergy is a success. I mailed 280 clergy of whom 102 have accepted and 62 sent apologies. One man, who says he is not gay but received an invite, rang me and said, 'I oppose everything you stand for.' When Michael Burgess left the St Albans diocese to come to London Eric James commented, 'Thank God we have thrown that cat over the wall.'

13 November 1979. Frank Harvey, Archdeacon of London, asked me how many people attended services at St Botolph's, and I discover that over nine months the average was 41 on a Sunday; 11 on Monday; 8 Tuesday; 11 Wednesday; 7 Thursday and 9 Friday.

1 December 1979. Three years ago with Dan Jones and Tower Hamlets social workers I helped found *Kipper* which is a charity to help East End teenagers who kip on the streets. We have a hostel in Limehouse and until today a day centre in two of the four tunnels of our crypt. I'm the chair and had to tell everyone that we now need the room for our homeless work, so the centre is moving to the hostel.

16 December 1979. The fourth Carol Service for the gay community in London with around 300 there. Andrew Charity's orchestra once again adds greatly to the splendour of the evening.

25 January 1980. I went to Pentonville prison to visit Ray thanks to the chaplain letting me use his room, but he sits at his desk so I have to refer to Ray's partner Norman as Janet so no one will know what the relationship is. Difficult.

13 February 1980. I preached in St Paul's last Sunday afternoon about Naaman washing in the Jordan – we fear anything different. This morning I had an anonymous letter: 'St Botolph would be better Without you than Without Aldgate'. Poor Alan Webster looked grey and worn when he gave me tea afterwards. The Cathedral is such an unhappy place with all the residentiary canons warring with him. Dean Inge (pronounced as sting according to him) said that he felt like a mouse being watched by four cats.

15 February 1980. I always enjoy Sir John Cass's Founder's Day. Two hundred junior school children come to church together with the first years from the senior school (Cass Redcoat) in Stepney. All wear red feathers in their buttonholes or in their hair Red Indian style. This is because Cass died in 1718 whilst signing his will having had a fatal lung haemorrhage, so vomited blood over his quill pen. He had only signed two of the five sheets of the will leaving money to the school. Because he was childless a long legal battle began, and it was not until 1748 that the Cass Foundation was founded. Lady Cass took the school under her wing until she died, but then it had to close for ten years. Today, as always, the Lord Mayor arrived in red gown, fur, lace and tricorne hat. Sir Bernard and I meet him and take him in where Jim Thompson, Bishop of Stepney, preached an overlong sermon. All the under fives, who I seat on the carpet around Sir Bernard's chair, went to sleep, as did Sir Bernard. Apparently the Queen has asked the Lord Mayor to wear a lounge suit for her

visit here in a fortnight's time, and he has replied that the Lord Mayor never wears a lounge suit.

17 February 1980. I went to *Smith of Smiths* at the Lyric Hammersmith. The script has all the best of Canon Sydney Smith's witticisms and Timothy West and Prunella Scales made the audience, which included +Gerald, roar with laughter. I especially liked: 'I never read a book before reviewing it. It prejudices one so,' and, 'In winter to go to St Paul's is certain death. My sentences are frozen as they come out of my mouth but are thawed in the course of the summer making strange noises and unexpected assertions in various parts of the church.' Queen Victoria regularly asked Lord Melbourne for Sydney's recent witticisms, and Sarah Siddons at their first meeting developed convulsions and had to be helped from the dining table. I would love to put on *The Smith of Smiths* as a charity do, and will write to the author Jane McCulloch of the English Chamber Theatre about it.

19 February 1980. Douglas Webster and Peter Lillingston give a party at their Wren house in Amen Court to celebrate their 25 years together. Douglas wrote to congratulate me after I did a broadcast in 1973 about the gay dilemma in the Church. We have been friends ever since, and lunch at the Athenaeum regularly. Bishop Gerald in his deep start-the-boat-race voice once asked me, 'Why don't you keep quiet? Douglas Webster doesn't keep talking about Peter.' I couldn't wait to get home and telephone Douglas to tell him. 'How does he know? How does he know?' cried Douglas. Everyone knows. I wish that Douglas would share his experiences with friends like Donald Coggan who is apparently 100% heterosexual and very happily married so finds it impossible to understand homosexuality. Douglas has an impeccable ecclesiastical pedigree, and his evangelical scholarship has earned him enormous respect.

28 February 1980. Bishop Gerald has had a letter complaining that Eric Heffer, the left-wing Liverpool MP, preached an anti-

Thatcher sermon at St Botolph's. In fact he gave a midday lecture. Then a Common Councilman complained that the Queen will see gay literature on our bookstall when she visits next week. To top it all *Private Eye* reports that the Bishop is under pressure to do something about 'Malcolm Johnson an outrageous character who has a crypt club for homosexualists.' +Gerald Londin tells me not to worry as the fattest files in his office are those of his best priests. 'I have occasionally read *Private Eye* in the House of Lords library – ignore it, I shall.'

1 March 1980. Dr Michael Perring of Harley Street does a training day for counsellors in our drawing room. As the subject is sexuality he begins by showing very explicit films – the hetero and lesbian ones churned my stomach. At one stage he asked us to line up – extreme gays near the poinsettias at one end of the room, extreme heterosexuals near the chrysanthemums at the other end. In fact the line of 30 people was not bunched at the ends but provided a sexual spectrum although I was next to the

Painting by Dan Jones 'The Last Supper at St Botolph's Aldgate' 1982. The gin bottle is mine.

HM the Queen visits St Botolph's, March 1970. I told her 'You never know what will happen next here'. Bishop Gerald Ellison on the right.

poinsettias.

8 March 1980. The Queen arrives at St Botolph's with a face of thunder because among the crowd of about 350 outside are some City Polytechnic students shouting slogans and waving banners. Looking like Queen Mary she icily asked me what it is all about, so I explain that the demonstration is aimed at the government not her; the students object to cutting grants for overseas students. Her face relaxes and we chat about the church until the service begins. 'The church is very well used, I hear.' The service (to commemorate Thomas Bray, rector of St Botolph's who founded SPCK and SPG) was unutterably boring and HM got very fidgety during Gary Bennett's tedious sermon. In the middle of it I heard the doorbell ring, and a minute later one of our congregation who has sold flowers in Petticoat Lane since the turn of the century made an entry into the gallery just

missing the drums and sat in the middle of the choir. On the way out HM asks who that 'splendid lady' is and I explain that Nellie Ellis now 80 was present at the siege of Sydney Street in 1911 and saw Mr Churchill the Home Secretary watching the police trying to find the Russians who had done the Houndsditch murders. At the ticket-only reception in the Cass school hall Nellie (no ticket and not smelling too fragrant) marched up to HM, curtsied and said, 'I'm Nellie Ellis.' 'I know you are,' said the Queen and chatted for some time. Fortunately a photographer got a photo of the two ladies. Sir Philip Moore, the Private Secretary, had suggested I present three helpers and two users of our homeless centre, and we get a super photo of her roaring with laughter when one of the helpers said he has been coming to the canteen since the year of the Christine Keeler scandal.

28 March 1980. Two of our friends, Howard and Hugh, give a gay evening party and Bridget, whose marriage has just ended, is staying with us so the boys invite her too. She looks ravishingly beautiful in a black dress, and is a great success. In the car on the way home she says what a waste it is that all those handsome men are homosexual.

8 April 1980. *Private Eye* reports that GCM is at St Botolph's. Will the Bishop take action?

6 May 1980. As well as being a first-class priest and counsellor John Lee has other tasks at St Botolph's. Recently one of our homeless men built a cardboard house around one of the wooden seats in the churchyard. Being a nice, friendly rector I did not move him on but asked if he would like me to find a hostel for him. 'Have you ever slept in a homeless hostel, Father? They are smelly and dirty.' So he stayed put, and the 'house' got bigger and bigger and he started to sublet, so he had to go. John had the terrible task of cleaning up the mess, which won him the Johnson Award for bravery.

28 June 1980. For first time I go on the Gay Pride March wearing a dog collar, and walk in the rain with the GCM banner

from Bressington Place, Victoria to Malet Street. I was very apprehensive but felt I must show at least one cleric has emerged from the closet. It is not much fun getting soaked, but as the son of an oilskin manufacturer I have never been able to complain. The family business, Johnson and Sons, began around 1860 and after Father retired as chairman its five factories were sold because Malcolm had decided not to be a businessman. By then there were 700 employees and Father had switched to plastics. The firm also made socks, shirts, overalls etc. Every year there would be a huge dance with famous bands like Geraldo and Ted Heath which was very good for my autograph book.

Sun 29 June 1980. A group of us have been considering how to demonstrate about the necessity of ordaining women in the C of E, and Robert suggested burning a cathedral down – perhaps Guildford? Eventually we decided to interrupt an ordination, so Alan Webster the Dean of St Paul's got front row tickets for eight people at the ordination today in the Cathedral. The group asked to see +Gerald for a few minutes to put their case but, although he thinks women's ordination will come one day, he refused. So after the laying on of hands Robert and Monica Furlong held up a banner ORDAIN WOMEN NOW and were unceremoniously bundled out of the Cathedral; Robert being punched three times by a tail-coated sidesman. The other demonstrators included Fr Ieuan Davies, Ian Ainsworth-Smith a hospital chaplain and Kath Burn. After my service at St Bots I joined them on the steps handing out leaflets and nails to the congregation as they left, saying, 'Remember the pain of those not being ordained today because they are women.' One man, accompanied by his wife and young daughter, said that he would like to punch me in the face, so I replied that his family must be very proud of him. At 3pm we had the Gay Pride Service at St Botolph's and 120 came.

30 June 1980. The Dean made the sidesman telephone Robert to apologise. The papers report it all on their front pages.

2 July 1980. An arrogant letter in *The Times* from Hugh Dawes,

the gay chaplain of Gonville and Caius, saying that the demon-strators represent the lunatic fringe, and strengthen his opposition to ordaining women. There 'is revulsion at worship being interrupted.' The women who took part and the priests 'who abetted them' are unfit for ordination. Pompous man.

4 July 1980. Monica Rejman, an eccentric old Polish member of the congregation who always comes in national dress, usually has a holiday each summer with the Sisters of Mercy in Clacton. It makes a change from her horrid Dickensian hostel.[42] This year I can't drive her there so put her on a train at Liverpool Street, and phone to ask the sisters to meet her as she is not able to look after herself. Today she was to return to London and the sisters put her on the train, but one of our staff forgot to meet her at Liverpool Street so she sat there in the carriage and went back to Clacton with the train. At 1pm I get a phone call from the Clacton stationmaster whom I ask to return her – rather like a parcel – so back she comes, smiling broadly.

16 July 1980. Stan Rowbotham takes me to the Parish Clerks Company dinner at the Tallow Chandlers Hall. It is an excruciat-ingly awful evening with inedible food, and men aping the twelve great Livery Companies. The Master wears a ridiculous embroidered hat and during the port they toast each other shouting out the parishes of which they are clerk – St Nickers in the Wardrobe – St Walter without Windows – St Mildred Bread Street – St Michael Crooked Lane – St Andrew Hubbard – St Martin Pomeroy.[43] Yuck.

21 August 1980. My first wedding of someone divorced. I know the couple, realise one of them has made a mistake which is forgivable, but feel profoundly uncomfortable during the service. Crazy really as I have already taken about 25 services of blessing for gay couples this year which are much more condemned by the Church.

2 October 1980. A Dickensian art dealer in Yarmouth, Harry Dyer, has died. He is one of the characters in my life because his

shop was a treasure trove of East Anglian paintings, and we have bought much of our collection from him, although it was not advisable to ask him to frame or do repairs because the canvases would disappear in a huge stack at the back of the shop. In his flat above Robert once picked up a study of waves and said, 'This looks like a Turner, Harry.' 'It is, Sir Robert.' Aged 60 he had married the young blonde bombshell of the Yarmouth Amateur Dramatics Society, but they had separate honeymoons (which intrigued my mother), and never lived together.

19 November 1980. As one of the Governors of the City Polytechnic I have been asked to help interview for a new Provost, and the obvious candidate of the 49 applicants is Michael Edwards, managing director of British Steel. It is an interesting career move for this lawyer who is modest, quiet and self-effacing. If he can deal with Russians and Yugoslavs he can deal with revolting students who recently have been inter- rupting our Court meetings. In the evening I chair a meeting of priests and rabbis at Golders Green Synagogue to discuss services of gay blessings. Some very interesting rabbis are there – Lionel Blue, David Smith, Colin Emmer and Harold Vallins. The lovely Dr Wendy Greengross is a great help in our discus- sions.

27 November 1980. The members of Gay AA are using our crypt and I go along to meet some of the members. The atmos- phere is friendly, but the smog from smoking is immense so if they don't die from booze the fags will get them.

1 December 1980. As Kipper have left the crypt for premises in Limehouse we now have all four tunnels for the homeless work. Daly Maxwell our gentle, loving senior social worker begins a day centre for 40 men and women chosen specially from the over 200 who come in the evenings. There is a programme of classes, discussions and outings, and each person has a key worker. The shared meal at lunchtime means everyone can meet together and about once a week I join in. Police cadets from

Hendon are among the volunteers as are a number of ordinands on placement from theological colleges.

13 December 1980. I was warming my backside in front of the hall fire in the Athenaeum when Ralph Richardson came and stood near me, waiting for a friend, as I was. I couldn't resist telling him what a profound effect his performance as a Norfolk vicar had had on me in the 1952 film *The Holly and the Ivy*.[44] His two daughters played by Celia Johnson (stay-at-home) and Margaret Leighton (naughty, lived abroad) came back to the vicarage for Christmas. What got me was the work the vicar was doing so, aged 16, I thought I'd like to do that. It was a sentimental film but not mawkish thanks to the actors. Sir Ralph was intrigued and I suspect that he had forgotten the film.

10 January 1981. Our Sunday congregation has grown considerably, and is now half straight, half gay; half men and half women. We still have our eccentrics like the 19 year old man who always arrives late wearing a not too clean, grey morning suit and carrying a cane. He times his entry to cause maximum disturbance, and the cane always falls to the floor as he sits down in the front pew. Then he turns round and stares at everyone. He lives in squalor with his mother in a large Whitechapel house, he on the top floor, she in the cellar. He is very bright and we managed to get him into a FE college. On a recent Sunday a lady arrived in a bridal dress, so afterwards on the front steps they made a handsome pair.

1 February 1981. We have three part-time secretaries who as nice as they are tend to overlap and cause problems so I have decided we need an administrator and Richard Basch has arrived. He will literally end my headaches; recently I wept with frustration and realised that I had made a big mistake – appointing social workers but no one to back us up administratively.

24 February 1981. I arranged a meeting for General Synod members in Church House on the gay issue, and 60 turned up for

sandwiches. Basil Moss, Provost of Birmingham who has written a book on sexual relationships, gave a talk about the Church changing its mind on this subject, but said that he had no pastoral experience, and anyway he found homosexual acts disgusting. I wanted to say I found heterosexual acts disgusting. Canon Douglas Webster chaired the meeting, and said that when the Lambeth Conference changed its mind on contraception he asked the Presiding Bishop in Japan what his bishops thought, and he said they are too old to be affected.

27 February 1981. The General Synod meeting in Westminster debates homosexuality, and Runcie says that he has now moved to the handicapped/disabled view. Does this mean we can park on double yellow lines? The Revd Bob Lewis, to his eternal shame, comes out as gay and then says that he 'is speaking from a dunghill... Homosexuality is a cheat.' I must get elected to the Synod to put things right.

24 March 1981. I go to the City Deanery party to say goodbye to Bishop Gerald Ellison[45] who tells us that everyone has three thoughts after retirement: 1) What an odd choice for my successor; 2) What a mess he's making; 3) Does it matter?[46] Who will be Bishop of London? Favourites are Colin James of Wakefield, then John Hapgood of Durham, then Graham Leonard of Truro.[47]

28 March 1981. I did last week's Good Cause on the radio, and 1,800 letters have arrived so far containing £12,485 including several £1 coins wrapped up from OAPs.

30 March 1981. Graham Leonard is to be Bishop of London which is bad news for me and I shall have a rough ride. On the radio today he said, 'Charity without principles is sentimentality.' There is now no chance at all of my being offered St Martin-in-the-Fields or anywhere else. Clifford Longley in *The Times* naughtily reports that Leonard was not one of the two names given to Mrs Thatcher. She added it as first choice. The Queen objected, but gave in. *Not the Church Times* a one-off eccle-

siastical *Private Eye* has a photo of Himmler on the front page above a heading: 'Dancing in the streets for London's new Bishop'. Among the adverts is one for 'A Charismatic Bondage Service' at St Botolph's.

Easter Sunday 1981. Standing at the seven sacrament font in Acle church I baptise my cousin Neil Heward's son, Mark. This was the church I ran out of in 1941, aged five, when the ancient lady organist suddenly started playing with a loud blast. I wouldn't even return for my favourite Aunt (Jean)'s wedding two years later. I stood outside. She is now Mark's grandmother and my daffy, adorable Aunt Dolly said to the parents, 'Why don't you go to the church and enjoy yourselves, I'll stay behind and look after the baby.'

13 April 1981. Terri, Harry Dyer's widow, has written to us asking if we would like the best paintings of Colin Burns[48] which were given as presents to Harry. They are stunning watercolours, and as the price is so low, we say yes. 'Harry would like you to have them,' she says. So they now join our SJ Batchelders, Edward Seagos, Owen Waters, WE Mayes,[49] Ian Houstons and other East Anglian painters' work on our walls.

9 May 1981. Our very dear friend, Derek Bowen, has been admitted to Addenbrooke's Hospital in Cambridge with a malignant brain tumour. An editor with the Cambridge University Press, he had been totally deafened when he trod on a mine in 1942. He is one of the very few saints that I have met, and was introduced to me several years ago by Norman Pittenger who thought that I and the SK group could help Derek come out of the closet. He certainly has done that, and we have always looked forward to his monthly weekend visits. Conversation at lunch parties is not easy because sometimes he doesn't realise that the conversation has moved on. Once we were talking about Jane Austen then switched to pornography. 'Jane Austen wouldn't like that,' said Derek about travelling by train. He is truly devout, fastidious in his faith and always wanting to do the

correct thing; so we were impressed when he, a Greek scholar and one of the editors of the New English Bible, wrote to the translators correcting their interpretation of the three texts referring to homosexuality. He is one of the only true celibates I have known; so many gay men including clergy say they are but are certainly not.

23 May 1981. Felt tearful all day as Anne Bowen has phoned to say that our dear Derek, her brother, is dying aged only 52.

24 May 1981. I drove with Robert to Cambridge to give Derek and Anne their communion at his bedside, and afterwards he says, 'You have changed my life,' and I burst into tears. He tells me that he has left me his books and a legacy.

28 May 1981. The clergy of Bournemouth have asked Richard Basch, our administrator, and me to talk to them about opening a day centre and possibly a hostel for the homeless, so this morning we do a double act before a large, attentive audience. Last night we stayed in a gay hotel owned by Frank and Graham, two friends of mine. In the middle of the night all hell was let loose and I thought that the police were raiding this den of iniquity, but I got an explanation over breakfast this morning. An elderly guest had picked up a rent boy, agreed a price and brought him to the hotel where the man's partner wanted to be included as well. The haggling over a new price caused all the noise.

3 June 1981. Derek's funeral at Little St Mary's where he worshipped, sitting in the front pew with his huge earphones occasionally sending out shrieks and shrill notes. A full church, and despite undertakers' disapproval I arrange for Robert and three young Cambridge chaplains including Jim Cotter and Nick Roberts to carry him into the church. Fr Gerard Irvine, his confessor, preaches and, in his high-pitched staccato way, says that Derek will now be able to hear the trumpets on the other side. I did the committal and almost broke down as I shall miss him so much.

11 September 1981. We are in California on holiday and have been spending time with two elderly friends of John Hunter who is a retired priest living at Charterhouse and our lecturer at St Botolph's. Both men are multimillionaires and at one of their dinner parties we met two young gay men who invited us to stay with them. As we were in a motel we accepted with alacrity. They have a house in Burbank with a pool which I sit in all day as it is so hot. Fred Joerger, one of the older couple, was one of Walt Disney's architects so took us to see Disneyland. We went on all the rides and had a cold lobster lunch at the posh Club 33. On arrival the first stop was the Swiss Family Robinson tree with rooms up in the branches. Fred told Walt that no one would pay 35 cents to walk up it; Walt said, 'Build it' and now everyone queues to see it. The great mountain for the rollercoaster was built in sections, and as it was behind schedule its top was put on the night before the opening. When Fred arrived at dawn he realised it looked like a penis with two balls, so some changes were quickly made.

15 September 1981. We drove in our hired Buick white Skylark to visit Alice Callaghan, a woman priest who worked at St Botolph's last year. She is an assistant priest at All Saints Pasadena which is a wealthy Episcopalian parish with an annual budget of over a million dollars, and 600 in church on Sunday. Her vicar, George Regas,[50] is a charming 'fancy' rector and backs her work among the very poor families in downtown Los Angeles. Alice discovered that one of the cheap 'hotels', which are really doss houses, for families is owned by a member of the congregation, so she went to see his wife. No changes yet.

12 October 1981. Clive and David have twice come from Portsmouth to see me about their Service of Blessing and today came with their parents for the ceremony. Surprise, surprise because Clive's parents tell me I married them in St Mark's in 1963.

29 March 1982. I had circulated a photo of handsome young

Professor John Boswell[51] on the invitation to today's Consultation for gay clergy so 110 members turned up – the largest attendance ever. He is young, very attractive and from Yale University. Last year in his popular book *Christianity, Social Tolerance, and Homosexuality: Gay People in Western Europe from the Beginning of the Christian Era to the Fourteenth Century*, he argued against 'the common idea that religious belief – Christian or other – has been the cause of intolerance in regard to gay people.' He also claimed the existence of a highly-developed 'gay subculture' in Western Europe from the mid-eleventh to the mid-twelfth century. He later spoke at an evening meeting we organised in Friends House. As he is staying with us I asked him if there was anyone in the audience I could invite for a drink, and perhaps something more. He chose Diarmaid MacCulloch, a 29 year old Oxford historian, but he had already hurried away.[52]

30 March 1982. I went to Wormwood Scrubs to see one of the founders of the Paedophile Information Exchange who was recently given two years for conspiring to corrupt public morals because the magazine had contact ads.[53] Someone told me he is in his cell for 23 hours a day in a special wing which sounds horrific so I thought that I would visit him. He told me that he has recently become an Anglican and we talked about *Honest to God*. Aged around 36 he has piercing blue eyes and he said that he had been befriended in prison by a man obsessed with martial arts.

2 April 1982. At Canterbury today Robert Runcie tells Eddie Erdman, chairman of the World of Property Housing whose new houses he was opening, that I should be the next Dean of St Paul's. Eddie, who is one of the patrons of our Appeal and also a prime mover in getting our hostel in Hackney built, once said that he would like me on his board of directors because I have a good business head. (My father would be thrilled to hear that.) Eddie, now 76, founded the large surveying firm which bears his name, and had some very important clients such as Sir Isaac

Wolfson. In the property market which attracts more than its fair share of rogues he has a great reputation for integrity based probably on his Christian Science beliefs.

10 April 1982. Trudie Eulenburg, our parish worker, phoned to say that her father, 103, has died, so I drove immediately to be with her at her house in Harrow. She has been bullied by him for all her life and when I said prayers by his corpse I was surprised to see how tiny he is. He owned the Eulenburg Music publishing business in Germany, but because he was a Jew had to leave it and flee to Switzerland in 1939. After the war, then aged 68, he started the business again in this country.

21 April 1982. I have been told by the ruling Junta of the Open Synod Group that they will not back my nomination for a by-election as I am too dicey. Brian Mountford is to be put forward instead. Bugger them, I shall wait until the full election in 1985, and not ask their backing.

12 May 1982. The *News of the World* runs several reports about gay literature on sale at St Botolph's, which causes a flurry of interest and headaches for me. I have to explain that GCM sell their literature in their tower office, and that the only pamphlets for sale in the church are academic lectures on the subject. Trevor Stephenson, a right-wing Common Councilman who is a governor of our primary school, makes trouble by attacking me in the head's study in front of our alderman Sir Bernard Waley-Cohen, whose only comment was, 'Is it illegal?' The Bishop comes to look and says that he thinks that the pamphlets are boring. Dennis Delderfield says parents in the school are complaining (the children come to church on Wednesday mornings). The Head and staff tell me they have had no comments made to them. This all worries me, but so far no trouble.

6 July 1982. I go with Deputy Iris Samuels to the Bishops' Banquet at Mansion House (I'm an escort agency). I lost count how many of the purple ones asked me what I was doing there,

but the prize went to one of the wives who kept asking me across the table why I'm not married. Over the turtle soup I gave a non-committal answer, but when she asked for the nth time during the cheese course I said, 'Because I'm gay and have had a partner for 14 years.' No more comments or conversation from her. Iris kept telling the Bishop of Northampton next to her that, 'Malcolm ought to be a bishop, he does wonderful work; how do you get to be a bishop?' The poor man muttered that she should write to the Appointments Secretary in Downing Street. I am very fond of Iris; she is the larger than life widow of Willie Samuels, the former Deputy, and says exactly what she thinks. For years she has championed the needs of the residents in Petticoat Square, and if the heating for their flats is causing trouble she always phones the Lord Mayor. Every year she holidays in Las Vegas where the Mayor entertains her, and she returns with stories of meeting Liberace. 'Of course, he's queer but I love him.' Same with me, I suspect.

7 July 1982. An Indian member of St Botolph's congregation is on trial at Snaresbrook for attempting to knife his MP, Mr O'Halloran, during a surgery. The MP's staff knocked the tiny Mr Putchay to the floor and put a chair on top of him, breaking a rib. The defence counsel is brilliant and makes the MP look a fool. I asked Mr Justice Butter if I might speak and told him that I considered Putchay mentally unstable and should be in a hostel. Up jumps the Defence: 'Are you psychiatrically qualified, Mr Johnson?' I tell him that I have been a priest for 20 years and know what I am talking about. In the end Mr Putchay is not guilty of GBH, but convicted of malicious wounding and confined to Brixton for medical reports.

22 July 1982. Robert and I are on holiday in California again, exchanging houses with Fred Fenton, vicar of St Augustine Santa Monica, and his wife Billie. As they are staying at Tredegar Square we are welcomed by Malcolm Boyd, an out gay priest and author of *Am I Running with You, God?* which has sold over

a million copies. He is bronzed, fit, 54 and was in films until he was ordained in 1955. He came out around 1978 with *Take Off the Masks*, and I particularly like his *Look Back in Joy* which is meditations on some of the men in his life. We met Fred Fenton and his wife Billie last year when we went to worship at St Augustine's, and as it was his tenth anniversary of being in the parish there were liturgical dances, harp playing etc. In his sermon he said that he owed his stability to one person – his therapist who stood up and took a bow. Poor Billie. Afterwards we met them over lunch and became friends. They arrived in London a few days before we left, so I took Fred to the Cass Foundation evening reception, and when I introduced him to the elderly formidable chairman, Archdeacon Michael Hodgins, he asked why the Church of England had no women priests. Michael, heavily closeted and severe, looked aghast. When we left he shook hands with Fred, then told me to: 'Take him out and burn him.'

1 August 1982. We are spending much time with our hosts of last year, Bill and Ken, the naughty boys as we call them. They are incredibly hospitable, and both are typical, focused Americans: working out daily, careful with diet, in therapy, well on the way to being millionaires. Only in their 30s, they have an open relationship and lots of sex fun (not with us). Yesterday I listened to all their achievements and meekly asked whether God has a place in their life? Answer, no. As they are lapsed Catholics I took them today to a Dignity[54] Mass where there were about 60 gays and lesbians in the congregation. They got lots of attention particularly from the gay priest, and they have decided to go every week.

21 October 1982. I visit Naomi Blake[55] the sculptress in her beautiful Highgate house and garden, which are stuffed full of her work. She is not at all off balance after her Auschwitz experiences and told me that after the camp was liberated she and other women walked through Poland to her home in Czechoslovakia. To avoid the attentions of Russian soldiers they wore shapeless

clothes, caps and huge boots. She wants to give a piece of sculpture to St Botolph's and I chose a figure *Sanctuary* of a crouched figure gaining strength from sitting against a wall. Many of our homeless men do the same. Lady Elizabeth Basset is there and I give her a lift home. She is one of the Queen Mother's elderly ladies-in-waiting and utterly charming.[56] She is not at all indiscreet, but says the guiding word in her Boss's vocabulary is *devoir*, duty. I congratulated her on her books of prayers, poetry etc such as *Love is My Meaning*.

12 November 1982. At last the three reredos panels are completed and are blessed today by the Bishop of London who looks a trifle uncomfortable particularly when Alison Limerick, a member of the congregation, does an exquisite dance before the altar. After John Piper's 'dartboard' design I asked Thetis Blacker to design them on the theme of 'Gateway' as we are at Aldgate and the altar is the place where heaven and earth meet in the sacrament of communion. She used the description of the Heavenly City in Revelation XXI as her inspiration and wrote to me:

> *We are each of us placed in this world and stand in one of the gates in our earthly city. We must look to the Heavenly Gate from where we stand in the earthly gate for we can only enter the Heavenly City from where we are. The centre panel shows the Heavenly City with its 12 different coloured foundations and the Tree of Life before it, and from its roots flows the River of Life so that we all may drink. The City is before us here and now if we only open our eyes to see it. The side panels contain angels guarding the gate holding Alpha and Omega.*

The hangings are made in a method of batik using dye and wax resist similar to the 16 banners Thetis created for Winchester Cathedral. A hanging pyx, designed by Juliet Pilkington in the shape of a dove, hangs above the altar which is now covered by frontals by Barbara Sansoni.[57]

21 November 1982. Funding our homeless work is a continual headache but strangely I enjoy it. We receive a grant from the City Corporation thanks to the good offices of Liz Crowther their Director of Social Work, but we recently heard that the GLC would give us £40,000; I had done a sales pitch at their offices. As six weeks had gone by Richard Basch, our very skilful administrator, phoned them to be told, 'We sent you a cheque and it has been cashed.' We checked all the various accounts with no success, so he rang them again to be told that it was amazing they were funding such an inefficient organisation. I then had a bright idea, and phoned Hereward Cooke of St Botolph Aldersgate and asked if he had heard from the GLC. 'Oh yes they have sent us a huge cheque for our roof repairs and we didn't even ask for it.' With incredible patience Richard told the GLC official what had happened. I suspect that Hereward has spent some of it.

22 November 1982. The Master of a City Livery Company gives the prizes away at Cass Redcoat School where I am Chair of governors, and he advises the East End teenagers, who are from some of the most deprived homes in London, not to have all their eggs in one basket, but to diversify and invest in property, stocks and shares. Jean Hayes, the Head, looks as though she might collapse but doesn't.

21 December 1982. John Clasper, who regularly visits the crypt, and who used to try and wreck the place is now a reformed character thanks to Toby his dog. The X-ray caravan recently visited St Botolph's and of the 70 men seen only John had TB. He wouldn't be parted from Toby to go into hospital so I agreed to take Toby to Mrs Curtis who lives in a Hackney prefab with six dogs and 25 cats. The smell is a knockout. Toby settles in, and she agrees to take him to Hackney Hospital every Sunday so John can look out of the window and see him.

10 February 1983. I drove through snow to say goodbye to Peter Elers in Addenbrooke's Hospital in Cambridge. Married

and gay he has pushed the gay Christian cause along, although he is just a little too flamboyant for my taste. We stayed at his rectory in Thaxted and Jill his gentle, loving, long-suffering wife who has brought up their children, told us not to move around in the four-poster bed too much because the mattress recently came off the frame and jackknifed trapping an elderly guest.

8 March 1983. I am met at the church door by an inarticulate Trudie and my loss of hearing doesn't help. 'Tredegar Square–terrible fire–died.' I immediately thought that Robert had died at home in a fire, but when we all had calmed down I heard that Mrs Jenny Thompson had been killed in a fire at her house opposite ours. It is a terrible tragedy as she has three children and a husband.

1 April 1983. I gave my all at the Good Friday Three Hours at St Paul Knightsbridge so was pleased that the Earl of Lauderdale in loud tweeds (one of four peers present) asked for a copy of my addresses. Yesterday the Mass of the Oils was held there presided over by Graham Leonard. David Skeoch, his stout, bossy chaplain bustled in, brushed Chris Courtauld the incumbent aside, and threw a white cloth over a table to put the plastic jars with frilly frocks containing the oils on. 'I thought it was a cookery demonstration,' said Chris. The Bishop was surrounded by dozens of good-looking young clergy serving him. When I asked where they came from Chris replied, 'Harrods.'

7 April 1983. CID men everywhere as thieves broke into the church last night and smashed open our armour-plated glass cabinet to steal our 1635 chalice and paten. The man who serviced the alarm last week said when he left that it was switched on. What he didn't say was that it was *not set*, so no alarm went off. Am very distressed and will sue the company.

24 April 1983. Buffet supper party at home for 33 gay guests and I included my churchwarden who has sent his resignation by letter. 'I meant it to arrive tomorrow.' It is a relief for me as it

is time for someone else to have a go. He has not been loyal and went to complain about me to the Archdeacon.

27 April 1983. I have a long talk about my future with our splendid Archdeacon of London Frank Harvey who describes himself as, 'A thug who says his prayers.' The wardens have complained about me behind my back, and he is not at all bothered. He tells me to look for a job when I go to America not because I am suspect but because I have had two posts near the centre of London and I would enjoy the Episcopal Church. Someone has already said that I have an American style of ministry. If I am thinking of going he suggests that I appoint a Director of the homeless work because no one could do the two jobs I do.

20 June 1983. Priscilla and Graham Leonard came to supper with Robert and me. We were very apprehensive but we have also invited Michael[58] and Rosemary Edwards, Thetis Blacker and Marybel Moore. Food and drinks were provided by our friend Paul, and we began with drinks in the garden surrounded by syringa scents. Robert in considering the guest list asked me if Leonard is a tit or bum man and I felt I could hardly phone London House and ask; so we had one lady of each. The atmosphere was a little sticky to begin with, but when our cats made a stately entrance the ice was broken because Priscilla adores cats. She and the Bishop didn't leave until 11pm keeping poor Fred the chauffeur waiting. Thetis says, 'You and Robert have created a little patch of Paradise in Tredegar Square.'

8 September 1983. Monica Rejman died this morning. I anointed her yesterday in Guys and will take the funeral. She put me down as her next of kin.

12 September 1983. I am at Virginia Seminary for a 6-week sabbatical Course. According to our tutor the motto is: 'We don't know where we are going, but we will get you there.' The college is on high ground several miles south of Washington DC and they offer 14 free fellowships each year. John Harper, the urbane

sophisticated rector of 'the president's church' opposite the White House suggested it for me. He loves coming to England with his long-suffering wife to preach in all the right places. A friend of Runcie, he has raised £2m for Canterbury Cathedral. He took me to a meeting of Alcoholics Anonymous which has kept him on track. He has known eight presidents. At the Seminary I found that apart from Professor Reginald Fuller's lectures on the Pastoral Epistles the academic input was thin because the emphasis was on sharing experiences. The first weekend was on 'Human Interaction', and we did a Myers Briggs test showing that I am ENFJ – not very flexible and therefore do not like changing agendas. I jump to conclusions too quickly but am sensitive to my and other people's feelings, fairly creative and imaginative. It is all rather like visiting a palmist at the end of the pier. I also did a hysterically funny assessment of what my gifts and interests are in order to find out what jobs I would be good at. Military activities are just below art which is top, then comes religion and social service. I have little shared interests with craftsmen, engineers, scientists and system analysts, but would make a good interior decorator, beautician, photographer, speech pathologist, librarian and social worker (in that order), then lawyer.

18 September 1983. I have an interview with the Dean, Dick Reid, a courteous southern gentleman who has been here 25 years. I tell him that I cannot receive communion in the Seminary chapel because of the College's views on homosexuality. He feels that we are in an 'interim period' and says that he is confused on the subject, so prefers not to ask about a student's orientation. If they say they have a same sex partner that is unacceptable.

20 September 1983. I was standing on the steps of the Seminary when someone remarked, 'There goes a female mailperson.' I thought that he meant a transvestite.

1 October 1983. Because I am in America I am not at the Clergy Consultation; it is the first one I have missed. Members

invited their bishops (24), and eight turned up and nine sent apologies. I suspect that some members stayed away rather than be seen. When I greeted people at the last meeting I said that it was similar to arriving in heaven. You have three surprises – the people you expect to be there aren't, the people you do not expect to be there are, and thirdly you're there.

7 October 1983. I flew to Hartford, Connecticut, and as we arrived it seemed as though the forests were on fire, but it was the autumn colours and quite breathtaking. I stay two nights with our good pal Clinton Jones who has invited me to preach at Hartford Cathedral. He is the canon pastor there and a trained sex therapist, specialising in transgender and homosexuality. Inevitably he is beginning to counsel young men with HIV, and I have learnt so much from him. Mutual masturbation is safe, hooray, and condoms are a must. He told me that an old lady came to see him, walking with a cane, and asked how one caught the virus. It is usually caught by homosexuals, he said. 'That's my brother,' she said, 'he's 89.' 'I meant promiscuous homosexuals,' said Clinton. 'That's my brother.'

9 October 1983. Clinton and his partner Kenny, who looks like Liberace and is a pianist, are the most hospitable people I know and we have had splendid parties. Last night they suggest that I stay with a handsome young Italian American I have met. Lucky me.

20 October 1983. I fly back to London today. I have been very homesick, missing Robert, and I have found the introspection of the course rather trying. Thank goodness I escaped for four weekends – on one to preach at Hartford to a congregation of 240, I also took a day conference for the diocese of Maryland on sexuality and spirituality, and then preached at Old St Paul's in Baltimore. The six weeks only cost me £1,787 and I had several grants etc.

21 October 1983. I am so very pleased to be back with Robert, and shall never go away for so long again. We celebrate with

supper at the Good Friends Chinese restaurant in Salmon Lane, Limehouse – one of the few reminders of the Chinese who settled here.

21 December 1983. A shabby cardboard box arrives through the post which I thought might contain socks for our homeless, but inside was the stolen church silver. I told the *Evening Standard*, 'God bless the burglars,' and it made Radio 4 and *The Times*.

24 December 1983. I take the Midnight Communion with Fr Eammon Rafety for the homeless charity Crisis who this year is welcoming hundreds at a huge warehouse in Vauxhall. He insists on separate altars and separate consecration prayers, but I mouth his prayer and then we each communicate 'our' people. Why is it we Anglicans always have to kowtow to Roman Catholics? Lots of the men gather round and sing the carols a little too lustily, so it is a rather noisy service.

1 January 1984. About once a month I preach at one of our 200 supporting parishes who regularly send us goodies and cash. It is an educational project because few know why so many are on

Lobbying Sir George Young, Minister of Housing, 1982.

the streets. A minority have psychiatric problems but for most a combination of events has pushed them down the slippery slope – the loss of a job, the death or divorce of a spouse, a tendency to use booze or drugs. The way our society is ordered does not help and I feel very angry (and say so) that the Thatcher government is selling council houses without using the money to build more.

The ordinary world collapses for homeless people and everything is focused on getting through the next 24 hours. They are

Princess Alexandra opens Park Lodge, February 1984.

not welcome in doctors' surgeries; that is why we have a doctor and chiropodist on duty in the evenings. These are among our 60 volunteers who are a marvellous crowd, and tomorrow we have one of our training days for them which I always enjoy.

14 February 1984. Princess Alexandra opens Park Lodge, our first hostel in Hackney which has taken hours of my time working with the World of Property Housing Trust. It houses 22 homeless men who each have a furnished bedsit, kitchen and bathroom. Our supporters raised the money for these, but there were a series of fires which we were told were an inside job.

Which of our residents was to blame? I took some advice before interviewing all the residents to see if any had a grudge, or needed attention or had any history of arson. We drew a blank. Two days ago the common room was torched and I phoned the Princess' office who said that she still wanted to come, so I walked down the road to Goochi's, a nightclub, and asked the two owners if we could use their premises. They agreed not to charge us, and the ladies of the local parish laid on a sumptuous tea for our 100 guests. The Princess spoke to everyone and it all went swimmingly with the Bishops of London and Stepney present together with the local mayor 'Call me Bella'.

23 February 1984. I had over an hour with Bishop Graham at London House discussing my future. When you stop him talking about himself he can be helpful and charming, and he suggests that I should be provost of one of the newer cathedrals, and will see what he can do. I mention working in America and he thinks it would be a mistake.

23 March 1984. Lady Donaldson, who fines you £1 if you call her Lady Mayoress, has me and 13 others to lunch at Mansion House. She says that she will come and wash up in the crypt, but I tell her that the clients would want a Lord Mayor to look like a Lord Mayor.

5 August 1984. A priest in south London phones to ask if I would see a young man for counselling. 'He is married but gay.' I agree to meet him. 'He likes older men, and, um, he likes clergymen.' Sounds interesting.

10 September 1984. The Wapping Group of Artists are again exhibiting in the church their paintings of the Thames and I must resist the urge to buy. Philip Groom, our tall handsome church-warden, is an artist so has purchased screens and lighting. Our art committee meets tonight and decides who is to show their work; they are Thetis Blacker, Peter Burman, Stanley Jones of the Curwen Studio and occasionally Nick Serota, Director of the Whitechapel Gallery, looks in.[59]

12 December 1984. An old lady has sent me six pairs of huge woolly socks for our clients so I take them with me to the Crisis Carol Service in Southwark Cathedral, and, as I have been asked to do the appeal from the pulpit, I ask the congregation to fill them with money. £1,060 comes in – the largest collection so far.

31 January 1985. Our friend Greg Richards, the prison chaplain, dies from an AIDS-related illness, and his photo is on the front page of most newspapers. His parents, who did not know that he was gay or ill, are flying from Australia. It is a very sad day, and to me ominous.

18 March 1985. An important 17th meeting of the Consultation at the University Church of Christ the King when 70 members meet with six Theological College principals, five other staff members and 20 diocesan directors of ordinands to discuss the problems of gay ordinands. Nothing but good can come from this sharing of experiences. We had to hire a hall in the nearby students union to get everyone in.

14 April 1985. A really splendid Easter Carol Service for the gay community at 6pm.

25 April 1985. Today is the centenary of the consecration of one of my heroes Edward King (1829–1910), Bishop of Lincoln. I first heard of him from two old ladies in Yarmouth who had been confirmed by him.

Most Saturdays they would watch him getting on the London train surrounded by all the porters, so no one else could get their cases carried. He always waved to them and they adored him. The vicar of Yarmouth Louis Baggott, who I first talked to about ordination, had been a barrister in Grantham and one day went to Lincoln for Evensong. He was a keen evangelical but told me that just seeing the saintly Bishop in the cathedral procession and hearing his sermon determined him to be ordained.

15 May 1985. Bishop Graham asks me to be Area Dean of the City which is a surprise, so I phone Archdeacon Frank Harvey who is his usual blunt self, 'There is no one else; two men have

turned it down.' So I tell the Bishop that I accept, but point out that he disagrees with me on certain issues, to which he replies, 'If I only gave jobs to people I agree with I would never be able to give anyone a job.'

29 May 1985. In the Mansion House we launch an appeal for money to fund our crypt extension scheme which will involve building a one-storey block next to the church, where there is at present a yard with a urinal known as Clochmerle. This morning a very handsome public schoolboy, John Reynolds, walked into the church and offered to be a full-time volunteer with no pay ('My parents can keep me') till he goes to Cambridge in eighteen months' time, so I put him on the door to charm money from the guests.

The Bishop is meant to talk about homelessness, but spends the time telling everyone how wonderful I am. 'Look around the room, what a tremendous cross section of people are here, all brought together by one man.' Very embarrassing. Percy Coleman, a former Area Dean of the City, at the same reception whispered to Victor Stock, 'Malcolm will never get preferment; he has taken too many pastoral initiatives.' Leslie Crowther[60] launched the appeal and showed great knowledge of homelessness. I liked him enormously; there was no celebrity gush to him.

15 June 1985. Last Sunday we had a BBC TV Appeal for our appeal, and we let the centre speak for itself. Hundreds of letters with gifts have arrived which will be answered by Leslie Bridgeman our Appeal Secretary who is unflappable – he was once Mayor of Redbridge and is now retired. He has to work in the side chapel because there is no room downstairs; that is one of the reasons for the appeal. Several pound coins were wrapped up in a note saying: 'From an OAP with a warm home'; and one widow sent her wedding ring. The prize letter came from Gorleston-on-Sea in which a gentleman told us he had enjoyed seeing Sarah our social worker on the screen, and would like to

marry her. He enclosed the times of buses from Aldgate to Great Yarmouth.

16 July 1985. As Dick Lucas, vicar of St Helen Bishopsgate, has said that he and his parish will take no part in deanery affairs now that I am Area Dean (because of my views on the gay issue) I went to see him and spent a chilling hour. I asked whether he would take the same stance if I married divorced people, taught that contraception is OK or advocated usury, but he would only focus on the gay issue. 'Nothing personal, my friend.' But it IS personal. I told him that I preach about God not homosexuality. 'That is why you are such a threat, you are respected in the City and everyone knows your views.' I looked at him, cold, formal, unmarried, and wondered what lay beneath the surface. He kept saying 'explain yourself' in a very patronising way.

1 August 1985. Basil Watson, vicar of the City Corporation's church, has also said that he will have nothing to do with the deanery whilst I am Area Dean, so I spend an hour with him. He is bloated and tired, and it transpires that he thought that I had arranged the demonstration in his church when Mrs Whitehouse spoke recently. 'Men in frocks and wearing lipstick danced in the aisle shouting gay slogans.' He refused to believe I had nothing to do with it. 'I'll make no trouble, but I will stay away.'[61]

8 September 1985. Bill and Ken from California are paying a second visit to us in Tredegar Square, and it is fun showing them the London sights and the mausoleum at Frogmore where Victoria and Albert are interred. They tell us they are HIV positive which is a blow.

20 September 1985. Our TV appeal raised £90,000. Amazing.[62]

8 October 1985. A friend comes to our Sunday service and over lunch afterwards tells me what a wonderful mixture the congregation is. 'I know that you have a transsexual there and it was lovely seeing her in her yellow dress and hat.' The trouble is he'd picked the wrong person: a woman who looks like a man in drag.

18 October 1985. I surprised myself by being elected by the

London clergy to the General Synod, coming second in the poll with 50 first votes, one behind the Anglo-Catholic John Broadhurst.

19 October 1985. +Graham sends for me, and I hurry to London House to be told that my article in *Christian* is causing great offence, and he has received complaints. Sir Timothy Hoare and other laymen from St Helen's objected to my saying to gay men that they should 'have fewer sex partners as few of us are called to celibacy.' I explained that in this era of HIV/AIDS I am not preaching promiscuity, but repeating the advice of the British Medical Association. I couldn't resist telling Graham about the member of St Helen's who had accosted Georgie Heskins after a funeral asking why she worked as a deaconess at a demon-infested place.

19 November 1985. I go to a service in Westminster Abbey to inaugurate the fourth General Synod and we process in full academic gear. The Queen arrives, and talks to us in Church House Assembly Hall afterwards. About 10 minutes into his sermon Alastair Haggart, Primus of the Scottish Episcopal Church, 'dries' and leaves the pulpit suddenly, all of us wondering if we had missed something, or whether he was ill. It later transpires that he had left the last four pages of his notes in the vestry.

24 December 1985. Only three fights at the Crisis Midnight Communion Service in a huge bus garage in Euston. I celebrate communion at a table in the middle of mattresses, and there are 120 communicants – volunteers and the homeless. We could have done with some incense.

1 January 1986. HIV/AIDS hangs over us like a black cloud. The Royal College of Nursing estimate that there will be 1m cases in 5 years. Last year I travelled to the States to talk to clergy and counsellors about how Christians should be responding, and when I returned I called together what has become known as the Ministers' Group to share experiences and plan events such as

services of healing. It's a marvellous mixture of hospital chaplains, maverick priests like Bill Kirkpatrick and me.

28 February 1986. I am now a Freeman of the City of London thanks to Peter Levene, our Alderman, and Alderman Sir Christopher Leaver[63] who gave me lunch after an archaic oath-swearing ceremony before the City Chamberlain, Bernard Harty. Over a glass of Madeira he made a pretty speech about my work among the poor. No longer can we drive sheep across London Bridge because the police objected, but I am handed a red leather-bound book, *Some Rules for the Conduct of Life: To which are added a Few Cautions for the Use of Such Freemen of London as Take Apprentices*. Amongst other things it tells me to 'be very cautious what sort of friendships and acquaintance' I contract, and at all times to keep my passions under my command. O dear!

2 March 1986. Work is progressing well on the building to the east of the church which will give us a large hall, offices and probably a doctor's surgery. Today Archbishop Runcie came to lunch at my suggestion in Sedgwick's, and I hijacked him afterwards to see the work in progress. He asked who removed all the bones and coffins and shrieked with laughter when I said, 'Necropolis Ltd.' They are an odd lot, very Dickensian.

12 March 1986. I went to St Helen's Bishopsgate to see Sir Timothy Hoare and six other laymen who gave me an inquisition hour. Georgie Heskins, our heavily pregnant parish deaconess, comes for moral support, and I thought I batted rather well particularly when Sir Timothy asked me how gay people see Evangelicals and I said, 'Like a black man looks at the Dutch Reformed Church.' He said, 'Ouch.'

5 April 1986. Georgie and John Holden, our priest counsellor, organise the first conference for clergy on AIDS/ HIV at King's College in the Strand. About 200 clergy and laity came to hear Prof Michael Adler explain the disease and what could be done. One of the other speakers was the Bishop of Edinburgh, Richard Holloway, who at the end of the day said that his vocabulary had

been widened – 'until now I thought that rimming and frottage were West Country solicitors.'

17 May 1986. I must be one of the few people who have a car space in the Square Mile. Each morning around 10am I sail down the Minories, turn left and park in a small area in front of an office building in Clare Street. This has below it the bones of the churchyard of Holy Trinity, Minories, an eighteenth century church bombed in 1940 and sold for a song in 1959. It had a chequered history as in the period between 1644 and 1695 over 32,000 clandestine marriages were held, the fees of which lined the incumbent's pocket.[64] Two years ago I was offered £47,000 for this small area of churchyard but selling a freehold in the City is foolishness.

12 July 1986. The workmen in the crypt dug part of the floor up in the western tunnel to discover coffins beneath so I ask one of them to jump down – carefully in case he went through the lid – and read the breastplate. It was Vink 1849 so it must have been one of the last interred there because burials finished in 1851.

13 July 1986. I receive a letter this morning from Major Vink in Coulsdon asking me if the burial register could tell him where his family vault is. I get on the phone immediately, and he and his wife come to peer in the hole at his ancestors. I asked what had made him write, and he sadly has no explanation.

21 July 1986. The Induction of the multi-talented Victor Stock as rector of St Mary-le-Bow, and Area Dean Johnson plays his part on a very hot evening. In the front row of the stalls are a large number of Masters of Livery Companies – the Worshipful Company of Corset Makers[65] etc. All were wearing fur-trimmed gowns and during Graham Leonard's stunningly boring sermon beginning, 'Beloved in Christ, I want to talk to you tonight about authority,' they all went to sleep leaning against each other looking like dormice. The Bishop hardly mentions Victor who has done terrific jobs in the London University Chaplaincy and St James Friern Barnet. He is fun to be with and I've known him

for years. Bow is in for an earthquake.[66]

18 August 1986. Our workmen have inadvertently broken into the vault beneath the front steps, so Richard Basch together with an Irish workman of huge proportions and I go in with torches to discover massive piles of skulls and bones together with 12 lead coffins. Bodies were buried in the churchyard for only ten years then dug up, so presumably this was a charnel house. The navvy began to get edgy, 'Father, do you think we should be in here?'

22 August 1986. I am on an East End committee to try and help with the HIV crisis in the area, and we hear that 400 people have now been diagnosed locally. I am 50 in a fortnight and feel very scared indeed.

20 September 1986. We always have a special Harvest Festival Service for our crypt clients and volunteers. John Cullen, a priest between jobs, has joined the crypt staff so I ask him to wear his scarlet Doctor of Divinity robes which are very impressive and fetching. Tonight was also exciting because I had just started a short address when someone shouted, 'What about Henry VIII?' I hadn't planned a dialogue sermon, but did my best. At the end of the service two very drunk men on either side of the aisle started abusing each other. 'You fucking Catholic.' 'You fucking Protestant.' The hymn had ended, and I could see that liturgical breakdown was imminent, so in my best Army officer voice I bellowed, 'Kneel for a blessing.' And they did.

25 September 1986. I was told to be at London House at 9.30, and having been given no explanation was trembling in my shoes. What have I done? It turned out that the London bishops wanted to discuss HIV/AIDS particularly amongst the clergy. +Graham asked me if the gay clergy were being more careful, i.e. celibate which threw me so I said that the younger, red-blooded ones were probably not. The bishops all talked at once, but at last I got a chance to speak so said that I thought that there are at least 200 gay/bisexual clergy in the diocese, and that I already knew three who were HIV positive. Guessing wildly but using DHSS

estimates I suggested that over the next three years it is possible there would be 14 affected by the virus, maybe more. I asked what could be done about early retirement, pension and medical care – would St Luke's Hospital for the clergy admit HIV-positive clergy? Tom Willesden who had said the most conservative comments, agreed to go to the Church Commissioners to discuss disability pensions, Graham Londin would approach St Luke's,[67] Jim Stepney to draw up pastoral guidelines including use of the chalice. The possibility of a redundant vicarage as a convalescent home was also mooted. I was enormously impressed by them all. 'We must not give in to hysteria and stand firm against prejudice.' The two gay bishops, Brian Masters of Edmonton and John Klyberg of Fulham, said nothing.

28 October 1986. Bishop Say of Rochester has told John Lee that I was 'much discussed at the Archbishop's meeting last week.' My work with AIDS was mentioned, and Say said, 'Malcolm is such a talented chap, surely there is something with greater responsibility he could do. We mustn't waste people like him.'

21 November 1986. Frank Harvey, Archdeacon of London, has died aged 56, and I was one of the pallbearers at his impressive, gloomy funeral in St Paul's Cathedral last week. We often talked about his and my future so I have lost a good friend who was reasonable in negotiations – as Area Dean I had to come to an agreement with him about the proceeds of sales of churchyards in the City. We eventually agreed that the parish gets the first £250,000 then the diocese takes 80%, and the Deanery gets the rest. Very useful and we have established a City Deanery Burial Ground Fund. Several people are suggesting that I be the new Archdeacon, but Graham sent for me and said he was sorry that he could not appoint me (no reason given but it is very obvious), and asked who I would recommend.

12 December 1986. The workmen have found a biscuit tin with a human head inside in the vault beneath the front steps. In

1852 it was discovered in the vaults beneath Holy Trinity Minories, but the hair and beard fell off. The word went round that it was the unfortunate Duke of Suffolk, father of Lady Jane Grey, both of whom were beheaded on Tower Hill nearby. Experts from the National Portrait Gallery thought that it looked like a painting in their care, but a surgeon from the nearby London Hospital pointed out that it had not been cleanly cut by an axe but hacked from the body probably with a small knife. For a time it was 'one of the amenities of Aldgate' and was put in a glass case for public perusal in St Botolph's sacristy. My predecessor found its gaze disturbing so interred it here.

7 January 1987. I have been visiting an incumbent who has AIDS since last October, and today I take his bishop, the admirable Mark Santer of Kensington, to visit him. With Tim Raphael the Archdeacon we work out a plan for his future – pension, date of departure, future housing etc. The two men are full of loving concern, and the priest is greatly comforted. The parish will be told that he has cancer, which is true.

10 January 1987. The Parochial Church Council discusses our work among the gay community. LGCM have used the tower room as an office for 11 years which has meant that I, our priest counsellor and the church staff have been able to meet and help hundreds of gay people. The PCC decided that they could stay, but some thought they might move in two years as the office is not suitable. We ask that the church address continues not to be used on their publicity because it would mean a large number of people turning up without an appointment and dear Mary our verger would panic making so much coffee. The Gay AA now meets here on Sundays, and we have had three special services each year for the gay community with around 300 coming to the Christmas Carol Service.

12 February 1987. A tired looking Runcie fields the questions in the General Synod on AIDS very well – 'the bedside of a dying man is not the place to work out your views on homosexuality.'

13 February 1987. I have got to know Fr Hugh Bishop recently, and he is taking a retreat for our congregation. Since jumping over the wall of his monastery at Mirfield in 1974 he has lived with Rob Towler and been in much demand as a spiritual director and retreat conductor. At one time he was a great advocate of celibacy so his departure when he was Superior sent shock waves through the community of monks and beyond. His TV programme when he talked openly about his new theological and psychological freedom sadly caused the brethren much pain.

1 March 1987. The crypt and church staff, now 14, met with the LGCM Committee today and we agreed they should stay although we need the tower room for our homeless work. Everyone agreed with the PCC that the link be formalised.

3 March 1987. Last week I held a dinner party in St Botolph Bishopsgate Hall for the City clergy and their wives, and had a cabaret. Alan and Margaret Webster came and wrote:

Hurrah Hurrah for the City Dean
Divisions are boring, destructive and mean
Let's have a party, all hail and hearty
Three cheers for the City Dean.

6 March 1987. The Bishop tells me two men have turned the Archdeaconry down. One has a live-in male lover – doesn't Graham know?

14 April 1987. The wardens and I have sent the Tenancy Agreement received yesterday to LGCM for their approval.

Easter Tuesday 1987. I preach at Bishop Mark Santer's insistence at the requiem for the West London priest who has died from HIV/AIDS. His parishioners did not know the full story, and I gather felt deeply hurt that he kept them away at the end.

23 April 1987. Bishop Bill Swing of California is here with his wife Mary at the invitation of the Ministers' Group to teach us more about HIV. They are staying with us at Tredegar Square

and I am immensely impressed how he, a conservative Virginian, has faced the challenge in a diocese where most parishes have people dying with AIDS-related illnesses. Seven reporters turned up for the press conference where he was asked about his fellow bishops. 'Sometimes I want to say to them that God became man, why don't you try it'?'

24 April 1987. Bill Swing speaks to 100 clergy at the Consultation and gets a standing ovation at the end of the day. He told me, 'You're working my fanny off.' I explained that the word means something different on this side of the Atlantic.

26 April 1987. Bill speaks on Radio 4 having spoken to a large conference in Central Hall yesterday. Two hundred came today to a Service of Hope and Healing we had arranged at St Marylebone later. When we got home before Bill took Jack Daniel's whiskey to bed, I warn him that when he meets the London and Southwark bishops tomorrow Graham will say, 'Before we begin I want to say something about this subject.' On no account let him because he will talk for an hour.

27 April 1987. Sure enough Graham tries to hijack the session, but Bill is too quick for him – 'We will have questions at the end.' The bishops apparently spent a lot of time discussing gay clergy, and agreed to meet again at the Lambeth Conference next year. I like Bill[68] very much, and make sure that there is always a good supply of Jack Daniel's for him.

I speak at an Athenaeum dinner on 'The Spiritual Motivation behind Modern and Historical Altruism'. God knows what that means. About 70 members turned up to hear me tell them, and Derek Pattinson chaired it.

28 April 1987. I flew to Boston to take part in the 'Ministry in much visited churches' conference arranged by Peter Delaney, vicar of All Hallows by the Tower and Bob Golledge, the large and noisy rector of the Old North Church in Boston. I played truant and drove through heavy snow to speak at a service for those affected by HIV/AIDS held in the Arlington Unitarian

church, full of box pews. The minister, Victor Carpenter, didn't mention God but encouraged us to 'heal each other.' AIDS walks with me daily and I am terrified of getting the symptoms.

29 April 1987. The day is spent discussing with cardinal rectors[69] like Dick May of Trinity, Wall Street and Jim Trimble of Old Christ Church, Philadelphia our common problems – raising money, caring for historic churches etc. Nice barbed comment – 'They keep the furniture, we keep the faith.' The conference ends with a splendid dinner and amusing speaker. He had been to a Rotary Club and after he had spoken the treasurer said, 'Please give more money, so that next year we can have better speakers.'

30 April 1987. Geoffrey Dickens, Tory MP for Littleborough and Saddleworth tells the *Evening Standard* that he and members of Childwatch visited the LGCM office and 'found it to be absolutely full of explicit literature on gay and lesbian love and paedophilia.' He 'felt physically sick,' and said homosexuals should not be ordained because they would be incapable of keeping their hands off the choirboys. Sometime ago LGCM stopped stocking *The Joy of Gay Sex* so presumably he is referring to the Terrence Higgins Trust safe sex leaflets. Another book he saw was Parker Rossman's book which is an academic study of pederasty.

1 May 1987. The Bishop has appointed George Cassidy as the new Archdeacon. The Bishop gleefully tells me, 'George is ideal; he has been a town planner.'[70] He is the evangelical vicar of St Paul Portman Square, which is about to close.

6 May 1987. Today I arrived back from the States having visited Hartford and New York to pick various people's brains, including Bill Doubleday at the General Theological Seminary about the ministry to those with the virus. Bill seemed worn out by it all.

17 May 1987. Whilst I was in the States several newspapers mentioned that LGCM is in the tower and Douglas Hughes, the Chair of the Sir John Cass's Foundation, has written to me saying

that he is 'disturbed' that 'one of the papers might mention in some tenuous way the Cass Foundation.' He adds 'homosexuality in any form is totally abhorrent to my understanding of Christian teaching' and that he would be delighted if LGCM vacate the Tower.

20 May 1987. Our Alderman, Peter Levene, warmly responds to my letter telling him about the recent publicity, and does not seem very bothered, but agrees that the LGCM literature should be in their office and not in church, even if it is too academic and boring for the schoolchildren. He really is a splendid man.

9 July 1987. The charming United Reformed Church surgeon Mr Lyn Evans tackles my hernia in St Luke's Hospital for the clergy in Fitzroy Square. I have a private room next to Trevor Huddleston – you meet a nice class of person in here.

10 July 1987. More people die from visitors than viruses, and I can see why. Today they let in Jose who was instructed by God to come to London from Peru and give a crucifix to Mr Johnson. He went into St Bride's yesterday and the verger sent him here. I thought that I was hallucinating and then hit on the idea of telling him, 'God wants you to take this crucifix to Peru and not come back.' It worked. I have been given flowers, fruit, books of prayers and hymns, talc, tissues, tapes, Dubonnet, soap, claret and magazines. I'm glad I am missing the General Synod in York because Fr Higton of Hawkwell is being mischievous – saying there are 20 priests with AIDS. He knows more than I do.

29 August 1987. I concelebrated in Chichester Cathedral and walked in procession with Gilbert Thurlow former Dean of Gloucester and one of the first to advise me about ordination when he was vicar of Yarmouth. He suggested then that every priest should try to be an expert in a particular field and keep up to date with its facts etc. I doubt if he realised that my two areas would be homelessness and homosexuality. He is a Trollopian figure because having been a minor canon at Norwich, he married the Dean's daughter, was given the best living in the

hands of the Dean and Chapter. Then he was made a residentiary canon of Norwich. However, he was not appointed to follow his father-in-law, but given the Deanery of Gloucester instead. He was an expert on architecture and campanology and an FSA. I like and respect him.

1 September 1987. Someone has rudely described the new Henry Moore 10-ton stone altar in St Stephen Walbrook as a piece of camembert, but it looked splendid when the Bishop consecrated it today and reopened the church after 20 years and £1,300,000 spent on repairs. Peter Palumbo gave most of it, and he donated some splendid 1920s vintage port for the communion service at which I was assisting as Area Dean. Unfortunately too much of it was consecrated so I had to go to the congregation and ask people to come and help us drink it up. What a waste.

22 September 1987. Our new building to the east of the church is opened today by the Lord Mayor, Sir David Rowe-Ham and we have named it the Hunter Room to commemorate our much loved lecturer John Hunter who has recently died.

23 September 1987. PC Donald Rumbelow, the expert on Jack the Ripper, gives a lunchtime talk in our local history series. The church is packed, even the galleries which made me wonder if he could do other lectures for us, 'Jack the Ripper and the Creed', 'Jack and the Church today'. He told us that at Judgement Day the Lord will ask the real Ripper to stand up, and a scruffy man in the back row who no one has ever heard of will get to his feet.

24 September 1987. Tom, a priest who has HIV, has joined the staff having seen +Graham four days ago. He has been out of the ministry for some time and of course no one will know his position except me, and he wants a Christian community to surround him until he dies.

28 September 1987. Robert and I are staying again in Los Angeles with Ken and Bill. We went to St Augustine's for the Sunday service and the organist played the British national anthem when Fred introduced us. Malcolm Boyd, now 64, is in

good form and in a newspaper article attacked the Pope's recent visit. 'He is trapped in a medieval vision of patriarchic control, monarchical trappings and misuse of vast funds for the glory of office while people go hungry and homeless. His unrealistic views on human sexuality have hurt and even harmed large numbers of men and women.' Who can quarrel with that?

4 October 1987. We were woken at 4am when the house shook violently and I grabbed Robert's hand. The hall clock fell over, china smashed and the chandeliers were swinging. It was a 0.5 earthquake and terrifying. Ken and Bill seemed used to it, and tell us that if it happens again we are to stand in the door frame as that will be the last to collapse.

10 October 1987. The *Sun*, *Star* and *Express* have photos of two girls from Reading I had taken a Service of Blessing for last week. A 'friend' had phoned the press to tell them where the reception was being held. 'The search is on to find the vicar', and I had several phone calls and a *Star* reporter on the church doorstep, but I should be given an Oscar for my air of bemusement. 'I have no idea what you mean.' The girls had approached three nearby priests, two didn't reply and one said that he was moving. So I came to the rescue.

11 October 1987. Tony Higton, the evangelical rector of Hawkwell in Essex has put down a Private Members Motion signed by 167 of the 550 members which will be discussed in the General Synod next month. The journalist Andrew Brown describes him as 'the Church of England's self-appointed scourge of heretics, Hindus and homosexuals.' He asks that the Synod affirm that sexual intercourse should only take place between men and women in marriage; that 'fornication, adultery and homosexual acts are sinful in all circumstances,' and asks that Christian leaders should be exemplary in all spheres of morality including sexual morality 'as a condition of being appointed to or remaining in office.' It is obvious that the hidden agenda is gay-bashing, so I put in a wrecking amendment which asks the Synod

to affirm the essentials of the biblical message that human love is a reflection of divine love and that all relationships should therefore be characterised by permanency and commitment.

10 November 1987. Two important Synod debates in two days. Today's is non-contentious and harmless – backing a church Report on AIDS. All the well-worn phrases are trotted out – compassion, understanding etc, and the usual 'affirming the Church's traditional teaching on chastity and fidelity in personal relationships.' The motion was carried unanimously but has no teeth, so in my speech I propose that local ecumenical task groups be formed, and that the Church appoint full-time workers. (I guess I'll have to do that myself.)

11 November 1987. It is my impression that General Synod members particularly the bishops are unhappy at being catapulted into Higton's debate with no preparatory report. I was called early in the debate, and said that the motion lacked faith, hope and love because it only addressed the first-time married and the promiscuous. In between are many people who need guidance not abuse. The splendid variety of God's creation, hetero to homo, is ignored and homosexuals, probably 4% of the population, need guidelines to help them live their lives not condemnation. My amendment was lost 46–325 with possibly 50 abstentions. The Synod then accepted the Bishops' Amendment which removed homosexual acts from the company of fornication and adultery. It said homosexual genital acts fall short of the ideal of a permanent married relationship. This prompted two gay friends to send me a note: 'We are going away for the weekend to fall short.'

12 November 1987. Bernard Levin in *The Times* says he had been overwhelmed by listening 'to an array of ordained clergymen chatting happily and knowledgeably about perversion and intercourse, condoms, genitals and masturbation.' He said that I had led the attack 'in a most exemplary demonstration of what Christian charity entails.' The tabloids

were not so kind with headlines 'Pulpit Poofs can stay' and 'Holy Homos escape ban'.

24 November 1987. I feel very bruised by the Synod but my mail has been 12–1 in favour of what I said. My prize goes to a retired priest in Sydling St Nicholas, who wrote, 'You appear to be over-preoccupied with sex which is not becoming in a priest. If my wife and I were a youngish married couple in your parish our reaction would be to keep away from you.'

25 November 1987. Archbishop Runcie asks Jim Cotter, Jeremy Younger and I to lunch at Lambeth to hear our views on homosexuality. I have always felt Runcie is a snob; he certainly had his Oxbridge favourites at Cuddesdon, and I did not warm to him today with his evenly balanced statements: 'On the one hand; on the other hand.' He once said that this was caused because at school he usually had to play fives by himself, and he certainly did not say anything definite today. Lindy, his wife, is a different cup of tea, as I found out when I had a room in the vicarage at Cuddesdon. Coffee breaks in the kitchen were great fun. She told me recently that when Robert was made Archbishop she went to buy an evening dress for state occasions and told the camp couturier that it was difficult because her husband wore purple watered silk. 'Oh how trendy,' he said.

28 November 1987. On 4 February I wrote to the Diocesan registrar asking him to prepare a faculty for LGCM to rent the tower room and today I received a letter today from Mr Faull, the London diocesan lawyer, asking me formally to apply.[71] As yet we have not heard what LGCM thinks of the Agreement I sent them at Easter. The Chancellor had learnt from the General Synod that LGCM were there without permission, and Faull hinted darkly that the Lord Mayor would be objecting. I had not realised until recently that a faculty is needed to rent a room in a church.

2 December 1987. I am told that I must apply for a faculty by 15th.

9 December 1987. John Underwood, our talented ecclesiastical lawyer, tells me that the Archdeacon of London will object to the faculty being granted, so I ring George Cassidy and ask to speak to him urgently. Strangely enough John represented my wife when we got an annulment of our marriage in 1969.

11 December 1987. The Archdeacon talks to me on the phone at 4pm, and it is clear in the 30 minute call that he wants the matter to come to court, does not think the press will be interested, and wants LGCM to leave because they are not a Christian organisation. Four times I begged him to see the damage that a Hearing would do to us all, and ask if we might talk the matter over face to face, and see if I could get LGCM to leave. I don't tell him that they are already thinking of doing this as the room is so small. I very foolishly said, 'If you want a fight I'll give you one.' He agreed to talk to the Bishop, and said that on Tuesday one of us must apply for the faculty. My PCC met this evening and agreed I should try to negotiate a way for LGCM to leave.

14 December 1987. I write to the Archdeacon asking for a meeting so that the implications of applying for a faculty are thought through. I said, 'I am not prevaricating.'

20 December 1987. No answer from the Archdeacon; his secretary says, 'He has nothing to add.' The PCC, after a long discussion, agrees to continue supporting LGCM, and John Underwood passes me a note: 'You are wonderfully blessed by a PCC of extraordinary quality.'

23 December 1987. Our Christmas party in the crypt and I invite the Sisters of Perpetual Indulgence. Four bearded members arrive in full nun gear including Sister Patricia of the Parting Cheeks and Sister Bridget over Troubled Waters. I got the impression that they were surprised that no one took much notice.[72]

30 December 1987. The PCC decide to continue their support for LGCM, 11 for, 5 against and 3 abstentions. They ask me to continue negotiations to avoid confrontation in court. So far the

only 'negotiations' have been one telephone call.

7 January 1988. Yesterday at the press conference to welcome the new theologically conservative, anti-women's ordination Dean of St Paul's, Eric Evans, a reporter asked if he realises that a City church is the HQ of LGCM. Cassidy replied, and said that he was taking steps to remove them. All the papers have this on their front page, and I am rung up at 7.20am for a comment. At 10am I read a statement in front of the cameras saying that 11 years ago GCM rented a room in our church tower, and a year ago the PCC decided to draw up a legal agreement and apply to the Chancellor for a faculty. This has been done and the only objection comes from Archdeacon Cassidy. The PCC feel that having this office on church premises: 'is a powerful symbol that gay people are welcome in the Church,' and should help them put their faith and sexuality together. I say that St Botolph's main work is with the homeless because 200–300 visit us each weekday for help. They are on the fringes of society, and so are homosexuals. I'm on the TV news for the rest of the day, and reporters crawl around the church, one of whom suggests that our young homeless are at risk.

9 January 1988. Having hardly slept, I go and buy all the papers and am surprised that they are supportive particularly the *Independent*. Our churchwardens decide to send the press release to all other wardens in the diocese.

10 January 1988. A letter arrives from a gentleman in Margate saying he and his wife are visiting London next week and as they are bisexuals and highly sexed they would like to meet gays and lesbians, preferably vicars and nuns.

15 January 1988. At the London Area Bishop's Council the members note that the faculty is lodged and I tell them that I am appalled the case is to be heard in court because no one will win. I suggest once again that we negotiate, but the Archdeacon says lawyer should speak to lawyer, and anyway Consistory Courts are part of his life as an archdeacon.

16 January 1988. A dowager from Knightsbridge proposes to the diocesan committee for Jewish-Christian Understanding that we no longer meet at St Botolph's as it would be damaged by association with us. She is outvoted. Sadly two of the patrons of our homeless centre have withdrawn because of recent events.

10 February 1988. As Area Dean of the Square Mile I pay a courtesy call on Eric Evans, the new Dean of St Paul's.[73] He is pleasant, affable, looks much older than 60 and doesn't mention the brouhaha at his press conference. His Thames Flammability Factor is, I think, very low indeed, and in the General Synod he achieved notoriety with a speech in the debate on the Scarman Report on police behaviour following the Brixton riots. 'In all my years as Archdeacon of Cheltenham, I have never come across a policeman being violent towards a black man.'[74]

20 February 1988. Because of all the recent uproar I went to seek the advice of Chancellor Garth Moore who is now one of the City clergy (at St Mary Abchurch). Could I be removed from St Botolph's? Now 82, he is the foremost canonist of today and I have always enjoyed our martinis together. After consideration he told me that I could be removed but asked whether the Bishop would want such a confrontation with all the publicity it would cause. It would also have to be proved I was not celibate, and he advised that Robert and I should have separate bedrooms and not talk about our relationship. I didn't tell him but felt that this was shutting the stable door after the horse has bolted. He himself is no stranger to controversy as he, as Chancellor of Southwark, in 1964 fell out in a spectacular fashion with Bishop Stockwood who then decided to preside over his own court.[75]

6 March 1988. Our second hostel, Scott Lodge, opens today for four men affected by HIV/AIDS. It is named after one of the men in Park Lodge who died of the virus recently.

1 April 1988. Graham Leonard's Newsletters are unutterably boring, and the current ones on the Ten Commandments are no exception, but last month he, as a postscript, had a swipe at St

Botolph's, so our lawyer challenged it. This month's gripping number has a back page statement from our point of view suggested by the Chancellor. It contains this – 'The Bishop mentions attempts to deal with the matter pastorally during 1987. It is not known to what he is referring, and the rector and church-wardens know of no such attempt.'

2 April 1988. I passed out in the church, and had difficulty in breathing so an ambulance took me to hospital, and after all sorts of tests I was told what I already know – stress is the cause. Many other crises have been facing me lately including vetoing a churchwarden at St Ethelburga's where I am priest in charge; sorting out difficulties at the hostel; and opposing some of the Cass governors who want to distance the Foundation from our two schools (I am chair of both). The doctor tells me to rest for 10 days.

14 April 1988. I go with our lawyer, John Underwood, to get Counsel's advice, and am told in no uncertain terms by Timothy Briden[76] that Chancellor Newsome, 78, would refuse a faculty not because he is very conservative (which he is) but because any controversial or divisive organisation cannot be allowed to rent rooms on consecrated ground. I then saw the Bishop who said we must seek settlement not withdrawal. I complained that the Archdeacon is too litigious, and tell him that the rector of Marylebone and others were also having problems. Twice the City clergy Chapter have asked the Archdeacon to meet them and discuss the matter, but he has not replied.

25 April 1988. Our lawyer asks the Chancellor for time to deal with the matter with due pastoral care, but is refused. What is surprising to me is that nearly all the City Chapter members are supporting me even if they disagree with my views. Chandos Morgan of St Margaret Lothbury, a former naval chaplain, told me, 'We trust your pastoral judgement; someone has to do this ministry.' Eric Jarvis of St Olave Hart Street came with me to the LGCM conference in Southampton to discuss the way ahead.

Both are married and both want to avoid confrontation.

26 April 1988. After last autumn's Synod debate the Trustees[77] in charge of Christ the King told me that the Consultation would no longer be welcome, but could have a service today providing we had the meeting elsewhere. So I booked a hall in the University of London Union across the street. What do they think we get up to? An orgy? The Irvingites, set up around 1832, are few in number today so they have allowed the University Chaplaincy to use their huge Gothic church in Gordon Square, and the Consultation has been meeting there for 12 years. The Catholic Apostolic Church expects the second coming of Christ to be imminent. Today's Consultation was therefore a gathering of very vulnerable men, and we spent much time discussing how we might support each other in the present ecclesiastical climate. Local groups will be formed, and our meetings will now have to be in the new hall of St Alban's Holborn thanks to the incumbent there, John Gaskell. John Lee, a trained group analyst, has agreed to convene a regular meeting to support members.

6 May 1988. George Newsome comes up the grand Athenaeum staircase as I come down. I resist – just – an urge to shove him down the stairs.

7 May 1988. A letter of support and a cheque arrives from Rowan Williams in Oxford who is to issue a press release on 'this wretched business'. In response to my request he offers to be a witness if the case comes to court.

9 May 1988. I am at a whole day's hearing before Chancellor Newsome, now 79, in Westminster which was a mixture of Toytown, Trollope and Alice in Wonderland. I ask for leave to withdraw the application (because I have been advised we cannot win). It was very humiliating. The Chancellor said, 'The rector must throw himself on the mercy of the Court; Much evil has flowed from his actions.' I suggest to him that as this is a Christian court it should be concerned with the pastoral responsibilities I have for the members of LGCM, but he is not

impressed. At 3.30 he asks if the proceedings could end soon because his train to Sevenoaks leaves at 5pm. In giving me leave to withdraw the application he rules that the PCC should pay the Archdeacon's costs (around £16,000),[78] and that I should evict LGCM by 30 September.[79] I am forbidden to discuss the case which, as I told the *Church Times*, was just as well because my views are unprintable. I realise that I am wrong and the Archdeacon is right, but I had hoped we could broker a deal for LGCM to leave without a confrontation in court with all the attendant publicity.

10 May 1988. The Princess Royal comes at our invitation to give a lunchtime lecture in St Botolph's on the Save the Children Fund. Tim O'Donovan, who lists royal engagements in *The Times* every January and is a director of Bain Clarkson, helps with the arrangements. Ten chairmen of local firms and all the members of our Business Houses Council turn up. She is a forceful speaker and very professional.

16 May 1988. Rowan's statement issued today says he is 'concerned as to what kind of pastoral care can be offered by the diocese both to the parish of St Botolph Aldgate and to homosexual Christians in London, when its public action seems to suggest a positive eagerness to humiliate and exclude those whom the parish and LGCM seek to help – and have helped, effectively and unobtrusively, for many years.' With support like that how can I be downcast? As the sergeant major when I was in the Norfolk's would say, 'You need guts VD – vigour and determination.'

20 May 1988. Peter Tatchell, young and good looking, came to see me today and asked if there is anything he can do to help me in the midst of our confrontation with the diocese. I was very impressed by him.

9 June 1988. My 25th anniversary of priesting and 400 fill the church for a service followed by a reception in the school. Many presents are given to me including an Edward Seago watercolour

and a cheque for £800. I read a spoof telegram from the Archdeacon: 'Best wishes on your retirement'. I was greatly touched that Canon Peter Ball came to represent the Chapter of St Paul's.

3 July 1988. Nearly all the *Church Times* letters about our case have been supportive and 70 London clergy have written to the Bishop deploring the way we have been treated. There is no doubt that some of the supporters of our homeless work have withdrawn their subscriptions but new ones have arrived. A parish in Wiltshire are concerned because the man who keeps them afloat financially threatens to withdraw if they continue to support us, and the vicar has recorded an interview with me. I failed to convince their PCC, so I write to the vicar suggesting that this man might try this tactic again now that he knows it works. The curate has written to say that he will send a personal donation. Sadly two of our patrons have withdrawn – Eddie Erdman and Ian Findlay.[80]

15 July 1988. *The Mail on Sunday* carries a three-page article on the scandal of the gay clergy, and says that City churches are 'pick up joints'. There is a photograph of Archdeacon Cassidy and some quotes from him so I went to his house to find out if he had given an interview. I could not see him, and he did not reply to my telephone messages.

17 July 1988. A director of Sedgwick's who is a keen Evangelical Christian went last week to see the chairman, Carel Mosselmans, to ask if the firm could stop supporting us because of recent events. He was told, 'When the Bishop sacks Malcolm I might listen to you, but not until then.'

22 July 1988. At the area deans' meeting I place the *Mail on Sunday* on the table, and ask the Bishop if the Archdeacon has given an interview. The Bishop loses his temper: 'This is a matter between you and George; you don't realise what strain he is under with hate mail, threats to his life etc.' No comment from George, but when I ask him what literature he has been showing

City incumbents he says, 'Oh they have been running to you, have they?' Presumably it was *Joy of Gay Sex* and Terrence Higgins' safe sex leaflets. Neither is on the church bookstall, although the latter certainly ought to be there to help save lives.

13 August 1988. Robert and I are holidaying at the San Domenico Hotel in Taormina, Sicily, and it is easy to see that it was once a convent as it has kept its cloisters with rooms off them. On Sunday we went to the Anglican church where an elderly priest, a Malcolm Muggeridge lookalike, harangued the 60 present about today's deadly sins. All good holiday stuff, especially wrapped in the 1662 liturgy.

16 August 1988. We visited Palermo and went in Monreale Cathedral on the lower slopes of a mountain overlooking the city. It dates from around 1180, is dusty and in need of repair, but has a glorious interior. The walls are covered with mosaics of saints and, behold, there is Thomas á Becket in an honoured position. On to the macabre catacombs of the Capuchins where dead bishops, priests and wealthy townspeople hang on the walls, dangling fully clothed on their hooks. Colonel Enea Di Giuliano is still wearing his 1800s French Bourbon uniform. There are thousands of corpses including several children, and many still have skin and hair. The bodies were embalmed by dipping them in arsenic or lime, but a more common method was by dehydration. Placed in the nearby cells for eight months they were then washed and dressed, and hung up. Gruesome.

30 August 1988. Our friend James Roose-Evans,[81] a polymath theatre director, writer and priest, gives us tickets for the first night of *The Best of Friends* which we greatly enjoy. It portrays the friendship between Bernard Shaw, Dame Laurentia McLachlan, Abbess of Stanbrook Abbey, and Sydney Cockerell, Director of the Fitzwilliam Museum in Cambridge. The latter is played by John Gielgud, now 84, so James as director is worried that lines may be crossed or lost. Fortunately Gielgud is a star and saves the day when he makes a mistake. Talking of raising money he

should have said, 'We are looking for a man with no children and lots of money,' but says, 'a man with lots of children and no money.' He corrected himself immediately by saying: 'But it would be better to find a man with no children and lots of money.'

5 September 1988. At the Guildhall Court today I am forced by the Chancellor to get an eviction order for LGCM. I am terrified that the press will be there, but the only person present is a man asleep in the back row who turned out to be a bailiff: 'Do you want them out today?' How have I coped with all this stress over the last year? Not too well. Fortunately there have been so many supportive letters but also some very hateful ones. The prize must go to a retired canon in Cheltenham fuming about buggery and bestiality. I replied asking how, after a lifetime of Christian spirituality, he could write such a letter to a fellow priest. I'm reminded of George Macleod telling me during one of his visits that unpopularity is OK, providing you don't inhale.

6 September 1988. Miss Margaret Marr, now 89 and daughter of the rector of St Botolph's 1899–1939, writes to say how much she admires my courage in standing up to the Archdeacon. 'It has made people think seriously about the needs and problems of LGCM.'

10 September 1988. A triumphant Service of Exodus at St Botolph's to mark LGCM moving to new offices in Oxford House, Bethnal Green. The special liturgy moved through the recognition of oppression and the need for reconciliation. Ken Leech preaches and the story is told in prayer, dance and song and the sharing of the Eucharistic meal – food for the journey. We moved out of the church and the LGCM statement of Conviction is read on the steps. The whole sorry affair need not have happened. At the very time when homosexuals need affirmation and acceptance Graham Leonard, George Cassidy and George Newsome have slammed the Church door in our face. May God

forgive them, I can't.

5 October 1988. I like Alan Paton's definition of liberalism in *Journey Continued*:

> A generosity of spirit, a tolerance of others, an attempt to comprehend otherness, a commitment to the rule of law, a high ideal of the worth and dignity of man, a repugnance of authoritarianism and a love of freedom.

24 October 1988. Recently I met Dr Ben Fletcher, Head of the Psychology Department at Hatfield Polytechnic, who has done a study of stress amongst the Anglican clergy. He wrote to 372 clergy and eventually 216 filled in his questionnaire. Today Ben spoke at the Consultation and got us to fill in a questionnaire from which he found that there was a high level of anxiety and depression in the group – not surprising. So we suggested he mail our 300 members to find some information and he agreed to do so.

30 October 1988. In a Sunday evening sermon 'Gay and Godly' at Great St Mary's, Cambridge I begin by saying, 'It is condemned. It is expressly forbidden in Scripture... Four General Councils forbid it, Luther and Zwingli weighed against it, and until recently it was distasteful to most people.' What is it? Lending money at interest. I naughtily ended with Richard Tauber's famous song by Franz Lehár:

> *Girls were made to love and kiss,*
> *And who am I to interfere with his?*
> *Am I ashamed to follow Nature's way?*
> *Can I be blamed if God has made me gay?*

David Connor,[82] the vicar, says he hasn't seen such a large congregation for a while, and walking up and down the aisle I much enjoyed the question time afterwards.

31 October 1988. The Area Deans Meeting broke up in chaos when the Bishop flounced out of the room saying, 'You have only got me for two more years.' I had questioned his eviction from St Benet's chaplaincy of the ecumenical, pro-women St Hilda Group. He said, 'I had to exert my authority.' I told him that many people in the country at large considered that the rule of law had replaced the rule of love in the London diocese. Exit bishop. I wonder how he justifies going to Tulsa in another bishop's diocese to ordain men who oppose women's ordination?

27 January 1989. I am preparing three talks for BBC World Service and the producer's brief is terrifying – 20 million will be listening. When I did this five years ago I got shoals of letters including one from a nun in Nigeria asking if I am the Malcolm Johnson who spent a year at the St Louis Convent school in 1946. Yes I am, and I owe my faith to those holy, dear sisters. The producer wants me to base the talks on a favourite book, and I have chosen Philip Toynbee's *Part of a Journey* because he tells how he finds God in his depressions, illnesses, marital life and even in Fleet Street.

2 February 1989. In the General Synod Mrs Muriel Curtis tries to get LGCM's entry in the C of E Year Book removed. I jump to my feet and say that we gays and lesbians have been insulted enough, and I am supported by Anglo-Catholic Dr Margaret Hewett wearing her usual flowered hat. She said that she disagreed with several societies listed in it, but didn't want them excluded. Mrs C also tried to get the members to deplore school material which said gay relationships were OK, and I said it was laughable to suggest people's orientation could be changed by reading a book. We win 140–132.

6 February 1989. We have eight for dinner today including our friends from Tallahassee, Florida, Betty and Paul Piccard. His mother Jeanette was one of the Philadelphia Seven and she preached at St Botolph's nine years ago giving me a nail to remind me she couldn't concelebrate. She still can't here. In

America a bishop decided he could wait no longer so unilaterally ordained the seven women as priests.

5 March 1989. I give lunch at the Athenaeum to Michael Mayne, the suave, urbane Dean of Westminster, and ask him if the Abbey would consider having a Book of Remembrance for the many young men who will die from AIDS/HIV. He declines because this would mean he would have to open similar books for people with other terminal illnesses, and anyway what made HIV so different? He did, however, suggest that he would hold an evening reception twice a year in the Jerusalem Chamber for those affected and their carers. Afterwards he would show us round the Abbey which, of course, would be closed. This really is a splendid idea and I accept and promise to provide names.[83] Thinking later about his question I realise that I should have replied that all the taboos of our society are heaped on someone with HIV – death, dying, disfigurement, drugs, disablement, loneliness, homosexuality and sexually transmitted diseases. The list is endless. Often those affected cannot talk to their family or employers, and if they are Christians they have an added burden of guilt and disapproval.

3 April 1989. Ben Fletcher came to the Consultation to give the results of his enquiries into the stress of our members. Three hundred ninety members were written to and 171 replied, which is, I guess, around 4% of all the Anglican clergy in England. Only one woman deacon is in this sample, and 36% come from the dioceses of London and Southwark. Thirty-four per cent were significantly depressed, which is serious because these are men who have gay friends and a support system. How much suffering there must be among those who did not reply, or who do not know about the Consultation? The average age was 45 with 35% under 40, and somewhat surprisingly a quarter said they lived with a partner. Seven per cent were heterosexually married, 51% were incumbents. We agreed that Cassell could publish the findings which are anonymous, and Channel Four will do a

documentary. However, I doubt very much if the Church authorities will take any notice.

2 May 1989. Peter Selby tells me that the Southwark bishops recently discussed buying new computers and someone suggested asking Archdeacon Cassidy for advice as he is an expert. Ronnie Bowlby, Bishop of Southwark, murmured, 'Not a good idea, he's not user friendly.'

3 June 1989. Littlewick Lodge, our third hostel in Hackney, was opened today by the Lord Mayor, Sir Christopher Collett. Park Lodge has already rehoused 70 people since it opened four years ago. New Islington and Hackney Housing Association have provided the house. The hostels are funded separately, and can survive financially by the rents charged. The crypt work costs £100,000 p.a. after we have received a grant from the City Corporation, but I quite enjoy raising money.

13 August 1989. The Angry Vicars' Group was formed in January to complain to Bishop Leonard and Archdeacon Cassidy about their way of working. The five of us, all incumbents,[84] have been summoned by the Archdeacon to a Consistory Court for various faculty irregularities, and we want to know why the Bishop rarely answers letters or phone calls. We feel an area bishop should be appointed for the City and Westminster. A month ago clergy and churchwardens had an hour with the Bishop and Archdeacon who listened and made no comments. Nothing has been done.

20 August 1989. A gazebo garlanded with roses is the ideal place at Cliveden for the service of blessing on the marriage of Kenneth Branagh and Emma Thompson. I have got to know them through Emma's godfather the theatre director Ron Eyre. We worked the Cranmer-style service out in his flat, and had a rehearsal two days ago in a hall near the Fortune Theatre. Emma, 30, is delightful, warm and friendly, but Kenneth, 28, is rather formal and distant with me. He wants to acknowledge the Creator, thank Him for the gift of loving, and make his vows

before Him. An orchestra plays, muscled security men look on whilst Sophie Thompson reads a Shakespeare sonnet, and Richard Briers reads from Pepys' *Diary*. Brian Blessed, a huge bear, is best man and at the splendid dinner afterwards proposes their health. In his speech he warns them of those who, through envy, will want 'to darkly destroy' the love that they share. The 100 guests included many stars, and apparently the day cost £30,000.[85]

21 August 1989. Brian Blessed was more right than he realised, because today's papers have headlines: 'Phoney Wedding, Fake Wedding. Actors play a part', because it transpires that Ken and Emma had not done what I asked, and gone to a Registry Office last week. I telephoned them both, and they have booked a slot at Camden Registry Office on Friday, but told the press that the ceremony will be abroad to put them off the scent. The press describe me as 'one of the most controversial vicars in England' and say 'senior clergy are stunned'. Ken told the press that as far as they are concerned the Cliveden ceremony was their marriage.

27 August 1989. John Lisners, a *News of the World* reporter, calls me Emma's 'oddball vicar' and berates me for saying that 'men should be allowed to marry EACH OTHER.'

28 August 1989. *Private Eye* has to get in on the act, so prints a *Service of Blessing for Celebrated Thespians Prior to Possible Holy Matrimony*:

Priest: 'Hello Luvs.'
Reading from *Look Back in Anger*
Reader: 'How was I?'
All: 'You were marvellous.'
Priest: 'Do you take this woman to be your unwedded wife?'
'I do.'
'Do you take this man to be the greatest actor of his generation?'
'He is.'

Priest: 'The Lord Olivier be with you.'
Producer: 'Cut. Take five, everyone.'

1 October 1989. Fr Hugh Bishop died today. I went to say goodbye to him a fortnight ago in his mansion flat near Victoria Station. He was weary and tired so I didn't stay long. Rob Tyler, his partner, told me that Lionel Blue had been and said the Jewish commendation prayers which Rob asked him to repeat the following day in front of TV cameras because he is producing a programme on death and dying.

21 December 1989. Fr Tom's funeral and we are not to mention HIV/AIDS because his mother does not want his brother to know the real story. Tom, who has been with us two years, was not likeable possibly because dementia unhinged him, but St Botolph's gave him a spiritual home for two years.

Christmas Day 1989. Mother, now 79, goes with Bert to the best hotel in Yarmouth for lunch. Just before going into the meal a taxi draws up and a very old lady gets out and sits in the lounge, ordering a sherry. No one talks to her, and at lunch she sits on her own. After lunch she has coffee in the lounge, then snoozes till tea time. Meanwhile a 12 year old boy is sitting at another table and orders tea, sandwiches and cakes. At 5pm a taxi arrives and the lady gets up and says, 'I've had a lovely day, thank you all. My son is abroad and has paid for me to come here. Thank you.' No one had spoken to her. Then when the waiter starts to collect payment for the tea, the boy, who'd had another plateful of cakes, gets up and bolts through the door. My mother tells me she thinks that one day he will either be the chairman of a big firm or in a prison cell.

26 December 1989. Two hundred homeless in the crypt today and we are all upset particularly Daly Maxwell, our super senior worker, because a man sleeping against the church door died last night. He wouldn't go to Crisis at Christmas so Daly had wrapped him in blankets.

3 January 1990. Our corner shop makes its customers including Bishop Jim pay for their newspapers in advance, and this morning scribbled on our *Times* was: 'Today is your last day'.

18 January 1990. There are reports today and yesterday in the *Independent* about the bishops' working party on homosexuality chaired by June Osborne.[86] I am one of the eight members who include Peter Coleman, Bishop of Crediton, Brother Bernard a Franciscan, John Gladwin[87] and David Atkinson.[88] We began work in the summer of 1986 before the Higton debate, and the bishops have now refused to publish our findings. The paper describes me as 'a widely admired homosexual priest'. We took a very liberal line which is not surprising because meetings were at our house and Robert provided lunch. I insisted that there should be a chapter on civil rights, but we did not advocate gay blessings as some think. All our hard work has been to no avail, and probably the only place to buy it will be Richard Kirker's LGCM stall in Bethnal Green market.

2 March 1990. I went into Wippells to order some clerical shirts, and after measuring me the camp assistant said, 'Well, Father, you're ordinary, normal. Most people in the Church wouldn't think so, but you are.'

4 March 1990. Ken, one of the boys in Los Angeles, phones to say that Bill has died. We are very upset and sad that he is so far away.

14 March 1990. In a biography of Archbishop Ramsey there is a nice story: 'I preached at St Alban's Holborn, very nice, very nice. The congregation consists of old ladies and young men. The old ladies love the young men, and the young men love each other.'

15 March 1990. The cost of clearing the bones from our south vault under the front steps will be around £115,000, but it has to be done as we are so short of space. Archdeacon George Cassidy has promised a sizeable grant from the City Churches Grants Committee of which I am a member.

23 March 1990. This is the first weekend conference Lionel Blue and I organise for those affected by HIV/AIDS, and is held at a convent in Nympsfield in Gloucestershire. Eighteen men, many of whom we know, arrive. Two months ago we had to meet the sisters to explain everything, and they said that they wanted a doctor present so Wendy Greengross who is on our committee joins us. The sisters have tried to explain to the staff there is no danger of infection, but two women decided not to be on duty. The theme of the weekend is 'Living, Loving, Believing', and Lionel begins on the Friday evening with the Kiddush meal followed by jokes told in his inimitable way. There is much pain, anger and laughter during the 48 hours we spend together. A nurse with HIV suggests some people don't want hugs, 'I've been hugged enough today.' One RC man was bowed down with guilt, and as we walked round Peter Scott's swan sanctuary at Slimbridge I hope I managed to clear some of it away. On the Saturday after dinner we have a social when people do their party pieces, and on Sunday morning I celebrate the Eucharist. People's courage in the face of this bastard disease is incredible.

10 April 1990. Roy Jenkins, Chancellor of Oxford University since 1987, came to visit Oxford House, Bethnal Green today. Peter Scott,[89] the gentle, generous millionaire who worships at St Bots and is responsible for me being a trustee, and the warden show him round, then bring him to an elegant lunch at a City Boardroom. We hope he might help raise money for the House, but after coffee he jumps up and says that he cannot help and heads for the door. Desperately I ask if he would get the chaplains together. 'Perhaps,' he says and bolts.[90] The trustees sat for a while in silence, quite flabbergasted.

11 May 1990. Bill Countryman from Berkeley Seminary spoke at our recent clergy Consultation. He came to lunch with me today at the Athenaeum, and said that I give the impression that my ministry is ending, which is not surprising because I was not shortlisted for Marylebone parish, and Graham Leonard has told

me that although he has spoken to Ronnie Bowlby, Bishop of Southwark, who reacted favourably, there is no chance of my being deputy provost in the Cathedral because Peter Penwarden (69) has no intention of retiring yet.

25 June 1990. A month ago I had a worried phone call from my friend Michael Gillingham who lives with Donald Findlay in the most exquisite 1720 house in Fournier Street, Spitalfields. They have demolished a Victorian extension at the back of the house and restored the building to its original splendour, filling it with appropriate furniture. The men working in their cellar had walked out because doors were locking and unlocking on their own, books were moving from one room to another, and knives were flying up to the ceiling. The men said that when they tore a cupboard down they felt a cold 'presence', and I certainly felt it myself. So armed with oil and holy water I said prayers for the removal of evil, and asked that if someone was stuck between this world and the next he or she be released to move on. I celebrated the Eucharist. Today I heard that all is well probably because one of the men who apparently was about to murder the other one had been removed from the site. The tension between them had apparently become intolerable, and this might explain the psychic energy moving books etc.

18 June 1990. Fifty-seven members of the congregation made a pilgrimage today to Under Hadstock church, Essex where Botolph is supposedly buried. Lettice Dawson and the villagers provided us with a sumptuous tea then we had Evensong. Botolph was a 7th century abbot in Suffolk known for his hospitality so became the patron saint of travellers – hence the four churches dedicated to him at the gates of the City of London. The church with its Norman pillars is a delight, but the chancel fell down in the late 18th century and the villagers carted the stones away in wheelbarrows to repair their cottages. In 1791 the Bishop of London wrote to the rector, 'Since I have been upon the Episcopal Bench I have known of no Instance of a Chancel being

Visit of Archbishop Tutu to the church and crypt, June 1990.
John Ewington chaired the meeting.

entirely taken away, nor have even heard of any, and I own it strikes my Mind as an Evident Impropriety; but I am open to further Information.'

22 June 1990. Desmond and Leah Tutu arrive for lunch with the Business Houses Council at 12, and then at 1pm I take him into the church during tumultuous applause to speak to 500 people cramming the pews, aisles and gallery. John Ewington presides, and Desmond thanks everyone for supporting the Anti-Apartheid Movement and warmly affirmed our own work. He answered lots of questions, then at 2pm the adults went out of the main doors, and our 200 Cass schoolchildren poured in the other doors with their teachers. They sang to him, then he danced around and got them dancing and singing for the people of South Africa. Lots of us were in tears. Afterwards I had to drive him through heavy traffic to Heathrow, and I got terribly worried as we had called on Trevor Huddleston and were late. 'Don't worry,' said the chaplain, 'they will hold the plane for him,' and they did.

29 August 1990. The workmen renovating the south vault have dug up a skeleton which turned out to be the remains of

Archbishop Runcie is amused that the firm clearing bones from the crypt was Necropolis Ltd, March 1987.

Mary Hague who died on 24 August 1812 aged 56. The skull with wig-like hair had become detached from the bones of the body, so I said a prayer and asked the men to re-inter it. A short while later one of them came to my study and told me that they had found a male skeleton and said, 'I have put them together so they should be happy now.'

1 September 1990. Ben Fletcher's book *Clergy Under Stress* is now published with a foreword by Jack Dominian. Predictably the study shows a much higher rate of depression and anxiety amongst gay clergy compared to straight clergy. He asks that the Church be a more caring employer, do more study on homosexuality and encourage committed same-sex relations. Ben says that the exercise has been a salutary one for him 'because I knew little about the Church of England, even less about homosexuals and nothing about homosexual clergy.'

7 September 1990. I say goodbye to my old pal Fr Fabian Cowper, a Benedictine monk dying in the Radcliffe Hospital, Oxford. It is his 59th birthday but he looks 90. A young nurse brings in a cake. He can hardly speak, but blesses me before I leave. I drove to London howling with rage and sadness.

8 October 1990. A boost to my morale because in the General Synod elections for the London Diocese I come top of the clergy poll with 103 first votes.

13 October 1990. Fabian dies. Robert and I are very distressed as he was responsible for introducing us in 1969.

20 October 1990. After a great deal of fund-raising I have appointed a Franciscan, Brother Colin Wilfred, as our HIV/AIDS pastoral worker. It will lighten my workload and I know he will be effective because he has been my spiritual director for several years. He has great insight and compassion, and an added bonus is that he is an expert on liturgy.

7 November 1990. Richard Briers, whom I met at Ken and Emma's wedding, has agreed to do the ITV Week's Good Cause for us, so I am very thrilled. He has visited the crypt to meet everyone and to help him decide what to say. The handsome young producer is Tim Knatchbull who is Mountbatten's grandson but I don't mention it nor, of course, does he.[91]

17 November 1990. I received a phone call yesterday from the secretary of Sir Peter Miller, chairman of Thomas Miller Ltd, who recently moved into the parish. Would I go to tea with him that afternoon? I said I was busy and had meetings (feeling a little miffed that I, a busy City rector, was given such short notice). 'It would be worth your while to come,' she said. When I arrived all the directors were there, and Sir Peter told me that they had seen the queue of homeless people outside the church at 5.30 so would I explain what was happening? I did my sales pitch balancing a cup of Earl Grey, and they listened attentively. This morning a cheque arrived for £40,000. That is serious money and I'll get Richard Briers to receive it at another tea party – in the crypt.

23 November 1990. Robert and I had a holiday in Cyprus last month which was splendid because a possible Gulf War meant that no other tourists were there. It was the first time I had been back to the island since 1956 when I served there as a subaltern with the Royal Norfolk Regiment in the fight against EOKA. On the last day of the holiday I drove to the military cemetery to pay my respects to those who had died, and I noticed the grave of Mr Williamson the local Consul who had been blown up by a parcel bomb. I helped with the funeral by making a list of the flowers,

and I remembered his young wife as I stood there. I prayed for her and wondered what had happened to her. Last week David Randall came to dinner, and when we talked about Cyprus he said that one of his CARA volunteers had lost her husband out there.[92] It turned out to be Heather Williamson, and today we had tea together at the Athenaeum. Charming and elegant, she never remarried, and is now a lay hospital chaplain, and has kept the letter I sent to her 34 years ago.

24 November 1990. Robert and I go to Fabian Cowper's Memorial Service in the huge, cold Gothic RC St James, Spanish Place. A long difficult sermon on *Eutrapelia* from fellow therapist Bo Stevenson did not warm the atmosphere, and *Be Still My Soul* to *Finlandia* reduced me to floods of tears.

20 December 1990. Stephen's funeral is held today at St Botolph's. Only 26, he had been the constant companion of my friend Colin who had recently taken him on holiday to Agadir. I knew that the handsome Stephen had AIDS so had visited them both in New Cross, and I liked him. The funeral was splendid with good music; a Rolls hearse and car brought down especially from Leicester and my first experience of a lady conductor with huge diamante earrings and a large black astrakhan hat. What could I say that would have any meaning? However, I did suggest that sometimes it takes suffering and misfortune to bring a person's best qualities to the surface.

Christmas Day 1990. A terrible blow, because just before beginning the service I'm told that a priest friend in Hackney, Simon Meigh, committed suicide at Barts Hospital yesterday by jumping off the roof. He had been told that he was HIV positive, but told no one. His vicar, Evan Jones, is an outstanding pastor and I feel angry, hurt and tearful that Simon didn't contact him or me. I try to cheer up for the Christmas lunch for 150 in the crypt which Daly always makes a happy occasion. It ends with songs, and to one of the homeless women I sing Stevie Wonder's *I Just Called to Say I Love You*, and she said, 'I bet I'm the first woman you've said that to.'

6 January 1991. Bishop Jim Thompson of Stepney has offered me the incumbency of St John Bethnal Green which is kind, but I have said no. Am I naughty to think that I am worth more? I preside over 14 staff here and also am responsible for the staff of the hostels.

24 January 1991. The south vault is finished and looks stunning, so we have a crypt tea party at which Sir Peter Miller hands over his huge cheque to Richard Briers. His TV Appeal raised £120,000, some of which will pay for a lift in Park Lodge.

12 February 1991. Ken dies in California so we are in mourning. His RC priest phoned us, and I tell him that I am so glad that the boys found a welcoming church.

27 February 1991. On this cold sunny morning I drove through the gorgeous Shropshire countryside to inter Dee Monaghan's ashes among the snowdrops in Loppington churchyard. His wife and daughter and about 40 others are there. Aged 69, a vet in Cambridge, eccentric, huge, lovable, he had been knocked down and killed by a car. In his blood-soaked diary given to me by the police was an entry saying that I was his executor, and I discovered that his will left everything to St Botolph's, so we shall modernise our centre's showers with his bequest. Dee belonged to LGCM, and among his papers I discovered that he convened the 'Fellowship of mature gays'. I wrote to the 90 members, some of whom I knew and hadn't realised were gay.

4 March 1991. I am having a minor operation in St Luke's Hospital for the Clergy, and the nurse asks why Robert is my next of kin. 'Because he has been my partner for 22 years.' 'I'll leave the space on the form blank then,' she says.

2 April 1991. A scrawny hen with ruffled feathers walked into the church this morning – she had obviously fallen off a lorry bound for the Petticoat Lane slaughterhouse. She was interviewed by a social worker and because of compassion (and her

inedibility) was taken for rehabilitation in Stepping Stones Farm in Stepney.

5 July 1991. Ken Leech, the Director of the Runnymede Trust and a famous writer and communicator, has joined us as our urban theologian. He and I managed to raise money so that he can help us and others think theologically about homelessness, drugs and race relations. To begin with I was apprehensive at having such a high-powered man on the team, but he has fitted in fine. At his first staff meeting he asked where Mary Everingham our verger/caretaker was and I said, 'She doesn't come to staff meetings, she wouldn't want to.' 'Have you asked her?' I went straightway and asked and she joined us. After all, she sees everyone who comes to the building so is a great asset.

2 August 1991. I make enquiries about two jobs outside church structures – Director of the Housing Associations Charitable Trust and Director of Crisis. I get nowhere on the first, but talked at length with someone about the second. Obviously I have loads of experience but they need someone in post by this Christmas and I can't leave here so quickly. Or can I? I suspect that deep down despite all the problems with the Church I want to remain a priest.[93] I'm proud that I gave an office in the church to Crisis at Christmas in 1975 – Jane Terry, the very capable chairman of the committee, staffed it and helped me think through the crypt work.

14 September 1991. Thank God Graham Leonard has retired. Before he arrived people told me that he was a pastor, but every time I went to see him with an agenda he talked nonstop about himself, and I had to try hard to get my queries answered.[94] David Hope is today enthroned in St Paul's as his successor. A month ago he telephoned me and asked to call in. I showed him round, then we had nearly an hour together in my study. 'Are you getting enough time off?' When he left I told him that this is the first time since my ordination in 1962 that my bishop has come to see how I am. In his sermon today the only parish he mentioned

was St Botolph's, which is very affirming, but I got a few black looks from my fellow clergy.

20 January 1992. The area bishopric of Stepney is vacant and I am on the committee to decide what sort of person we need. The new Archdeacon of Hackney, Clive Young,[95] is the chairman, and forbids us to discuss names, which infuriates me. He tells me that I am out of order. Why do the hierarchy treat us like children? Sydney Smith was right in saying that they like 'a dropping down deadness in their clergy.'

27 February 1992. 'Are you really a Princess?' asks one of our crypt clients in the kitchen. 'Yes,' says Princess Alexandra who is visiting the Centre. 'Do you enjoy it?' 'Very much.' Daly then brings her upstairs for a Thanksgiving Service in the church which is full to overflowing including the gallery. I meet her at the door and take her in. During the 30-minute service she listens to Graham and Richard telling Nerissa Jones, our forceful, talented deacon, what it is like to be homeless. Bishop George Appleton started the centre 30 years ago, so we are saying thank you.

21 April 1992. George Carey gives six of us lunch at Lambeth Palace to discuss the gay thing. Rowan Williams, Lady Margaret Professor comes from Oxford, Jack Nicholls,[96] Bishop of Lancaster, Elaine Jones, Sebastian Sandys, Jeffrey John and me. Runcie's very dishy waiters have been replaced by two mumsy ladies from the East End. In the session before lunch the Archbishop has a go at me for criticising him for persuading the publisher SPCK not to publish a book of prayers compiled by the theologian Liz Stuart for gays and lesbians. I stood my ground and said it was hardly a manual of gay sex. He appears not to have known many happy homosexuals, and said that it was 'a minority problem.' Unfortunately we disagreed among ourselves because although Jeffery was pushing monogamy, Sebastian referred to Tony Coxon's research of 2,000 gay men few of whom are physically faithful. I mention civil rights which went down

like a lead balloon. It was very good to have the fearsomely clever Rowan there.

26 April 1992. I go with Fr Damian, Minister General of the Franciscans and Mother Christine of the Nursing Sisters of St John the Divine to London House where David Hope hosts a meeting with the governors of the Royal Foundation of St Katharine who need a new Master. On the doorstep Damian offers a prayer but it doesn't work because the members under the chairmanship of Viscount Churchill seem unwelcoming and uninterested. I suspect that the Bishop is pushing them to accept me with the sisters and brothers. I feel very angry and depressed. Damian and Christine say they would only be interested if I am Master which is warming, and I say that I do not want a daffodil/primroses retreat house but one that looks at God in an urban setting.

27 May 1992. The Court at SK met, and I am told that they want me to live in which has never been part of the deal so I say no.

18 June 1992. It is obvious that the present Master of RFSK, Christopher Lowe, a monk of the Community of the Resurrection, Mirfield, is horrified that I might follow him. He shows me and the sisters and brothers round the house in a perfunctory way, and it is difficult to extract any information from him. In the garden Lord Churchill sits his cousin Sister Iona down and asks if she thinks that I will turn SK into a gay place. She is a fan of mine, so says NO.

3 July 1992. All the nuns, 15 of them, sit round their common room in Birmingham whilst I do a sales pitch for them to close their house in Vauxhall and move four sisters to St Katharine's. They listen attentively and give the go-ahead, even the oldies. On the way home I call in at Charlecote Park to see the artist Edmund Fairfax-Lucy whose family have owned it for generations. Now divorced, he lives in one wing in a slightly chaotic few rooms jumbled with antiques, dust and cats. I have always admired his

paintings at the Summer RA exhibition which are never for sale, and today he hedges and demurs at the ones I would love to have. 'My mother likes that one, that is one of my favourites etc, so I come away empty handed.

2 August 1992. Our fourth hostel, Corby Lodge named after Philip, opens today in Spitalfields with no fuss. My departure is taking all my energy.

27 September 1992. 'Soap Star's Gay Vows' screams the front page headline in the *News of the World* telling everyone that I, 'a homosexual's vicar', conducted a gay 'wedding' between the soap star of the TV show *Eldorado* Polly Perkins and her lover Jackie Raymen. This was in April 1982 and I defended myself strongly. 'It is blasphemous and wrong,' says my adversary Fr Tony Higton. This seems strange to me because we are talking about women who love one another, although now, sadly, they are splitting up – amicably.

2 October 1992. Gerald Ellison died yesterday, and in his *Independent* obituary Alan Webster salutes a man who had been an oarsman and naval chaplain but never rocked the boat. He was, says Alan, 'so confident in his own powers of leadership that he could afford to make daring appointments – Donald Reeves, Malcolm Johnson, Gonville Ffrench-Beytagh.[97] He searched for individuals committed to the community rather than to churchy trivia.' I owe Gerald a lot and will miss him. Every November since his retirement he has asked me to be his chaplain at the Festival of Remembrance in the Albert Hall.

25 October 1992. I preached to a full church in Miami on National AIDS Sunday. We are staying with Allan Stiffler, who is living with the virus, and his partner Bob, a lecturer, who is very loving to him. I met Allan, who was the librarian at the Episcopal Divinity School, thanks to Norman Pittenger ten years ago. Then we motored down to Key West crossing many bridges which connect the islands. Later whilst walking round the cemetery in Key West I see an inscription: 'I told you I was ill'.

27 November 1992. This evening was my farewell service at St Botolph's with a crowded church. At the end, having said goodbye to various representatives of schools, crypt etc, in silence I remove my chasuble, hand the church keys to the wardens and walk out in silence. A voice from one of the homeless men in the gallery says, 'Anyone got a fucking tissue?'

6 December 1992. A three-page article about me and my time at St Botolph's was printed in *The Guardian* a week ago. It is written by my friend Rupert Haselden, so is obviously very supportive, and I pull no punches. Predictably the mail is half hate and half very affirming. The former is well represented by a woman from the Isle of Man – 'Sodomites or gays live against the natural Order as ordained by the Lord God Almighty. They use their love participations through the organ of excreta contaminating the flesh and causing dire peril to the whole human race.' Bible quotes follow. 'Dare you meet God?' Meanwhile Dr David Hattersley of Wisbech with a long string of degrees writes, 'It sounds as if you have been struggling against various tides for a long while and are still swimming! You must have been a catalyst of hope for a lot of people. I admire your honesty.'

17 December 1992. I broadcast, which is repeated twice, on World Service, and use Scott Holland's 'If you believe in the Incarnation you believe in drains'. Drainage is still an issue in the Third World, and I went on to say that I felt the passion for social justice seems to have evaporated in the Church. Not, however, in the American Episcopal Church. When we stayed with Fred and Billie Fenton in Los Angeles Billie told me she would not be around the following day as she and other clergy wives and nuns were going to lay down in front of the Mayor's car to protest at his cruel comments on Hispanic immigrants. On air I suggested that our churches should be places of prayer and protest. We don't seem to possess the courage of the 90 year old who gave a talk recently at St Botolph's about her time as a suffragette. I asked her what she did for the cause – 'I set buildings on fire; I

made sure no one was inside then I torched them.'

19 January 1993. The sisters, brothers and I have moved into St Katharine's (I am permitted to live in my own house), and today the Archbishop's Appointment Secretary, Hector McClean, tall, lanky, gracious and a touch arrogant, came to see me to discuss the Crown Appointments Committee continuing to meet four times each year in the house. They meet to appoint diocesan bishops and want absolute secrecy, no one else in the house, and no reference to which diocese they are discussing. I got hotter and hotter under the collar as I detest the whole clandestine system, and eventually told him so. However, his geniality disarmed me, and I tell him that if he wants the 12 members to have sole occupancy for two nights then he must pay an extra £100. Eventually he agreed and I suppose we must lump it.

2 February 1993. I was among the robed clergy at an Induction today and walked in with Eric James to sit in a semicircle behind the altar. As we sat down he 'goosed' me – except it wasn't me but a senior evangelical cleric. I wondered why he'd said, 'Oh.'

4 February 1993. I have been stalked by a woman for nearly three years and it is rather trying. She is thin, gaunt and has a distracted air about her. She suddenly started attending every service at St Botolph's then began sitting in the gallery at the General Synod gazing at me during debates. She then came to all sorts of meetings where I was present and began giving me presents. She even joined LGCM. I tried to get to know her – not too well – and it transpired that she arrived in London three years ago when her bishop (John Yates of Gloucester) moved to work at Lambeth Palace. She has obviously transferred her affections to me so I wrote to the Bishop who rang me obviously delighted he is now off her visiting list. I asked how he had coped, and was told that he and his wife gave her tea at the Army and Navy once a month and that had shut her up. I'll try it. A psychiatrist tells me that she is suffering from De Clerambault's

Syndrome – erotomania, a mistaken belief someone is in love with you.

20 February 1993. My Installation by the bishops of London and Stepney as Master of St Katharine's, so I stride into the full chapel carrying my staff of office. After the reception as a cabaret I interview Eric James in full nineteenth century fig as Canon Sydney Smith. Jane McCulloch has given me permission to reduce her script *Smith of Smiths* to 40 minutes, and we have already performed it for various clerical audiences. All the witticisms are there, and I particularly like, 'The observance of the Church concerning feasts and fasts are tolerably well kept; the rich keep the feasts and the poor keep the fasts'; 'There are three sexes, men, women and clergy'; 'Marriage resembles a pair of shears, so joined that they cannot be separated, often moving in different directions, yet always punishing anyone who comes between them'.

3 May 1993. My stalker plan has worked. She and I meet in the crypt of St Martin's for an hour's chat over coffee every month and I don't see her except for Sunday services in between. I wrote to let Bishop Richard know in case she turns nasty, and a sympathetic letter came by return ending, 'I myself would draw the line at tea at the Army and Navy.'

10 May 1993. To St Paul's Grove Park, Chiswick for the funeral of Charles (Charalambos) Sofianos, 36, struck down by HIV. He was a tremendous extrovert, painter and last of David Randall's lovers. I sat in the choir next to Paul Bates, Canon of Westminster, and as Archbishop Gregorios of Thyateira wafted by I said, 'The Orthodox all look the same,' to which Paul said, 'Oh no, they are all quite different, but when they get up in the morning they put on a beard, black dress, tall hat and grab a silver-topped staff.' At the end of the service, which included Queen's *These are the Days of Our Lives*, we all spilled into the road to wave goodbye to the hearse before going into the vicarage for champagne.

5 June 1993. Gordon Gardiner, one of my closest friends, gives

a lunch at the Garrick in memory of his partner Jonathan whose funeral at St Bride's I took recently. Anne Evans was too upset to sing then, so sang today. The coffee room looked superb and I have decided to put a paragraph in my will saying that friends should lunch a month after my funeral. I am up for membership so hope that it will be here.

1 July 1993. Norry McCurry,[98] who was rector of St Dunstan Stepney 1973–85, died on the day I received a card from him asking me to call in to cheer him up. I telephoned Ruth who told me he had just expired. I was terribly upset as he was such fun to be with, and a great support to me on the conservative Sir John Cass's Foundation. He had a high-pitched shriek of a laugh, and lots of Irish blarney. 'Malcolm, that prayer you used was superb; please write it out for me.' He was to me a Pattern Priest, someone all his many curates and others could model themselves on. He had a marvellous sense of humour – sitting at the boring Cass Bursaries Committee he suddenly shoved in front of me an application he had filled out for a Mr Richard Whittington who wanted to move to London to do a Business Studies Course. The Cass clerk's comment was, 'Mr Whittington presented well but seems troubled by bells ringing in his head. We were surprised that he was accompanied at the interview by his cat.' When Norry gave a clergy party to say farewell to Trevor Huddleston as Bishop of Stepney he thought the punch was too weak so emptied a bottle of brandy into it not realising that Ruth had done the same. Trevor who doesn't drink was astounded that all the priests were squiffy, and several of them kissed him goodbye.

21 July 1993. The Queen Mum as Patron comes on a private visit at 5pm to St Katharine's with only the staff and governors present. I had phoned Clarence House to ask what tea she prefers, and there was a long silence then, 'Is there anything stronger on offer?' Three parts of gin to one of martini is the royal tipple, so I mix it in a rather large glass and hold it for her. She

chats so easily and told me to 'jolly up' the chapel which is gloomy, cold and bare.

8 September 1993. I mark my 57th birthday with a trip to the mountain monastery of Montserrat to see the Virgin who I share a birthday with. Robert and I are staying at Sitges, near Barcelona, and we arrive at the chapel just as 1,500 people crowd in to hear the famous choir who sing every day at noon. The priest then prays. It would be a good idea if St Paul's or the Abbey did this. I came here 25 years ago and prayed fervently asking the Virgin to make me heterosexual. Up till now I have been angry because my prayers were not answered (fine Mother she is) but they HAVE been answered for I have had 24 years with Robert who gives me all I need. At the mass I say thank you, and then remember all the young who have died recently.

12 September 1993. We flew home arriving 6pm and I went straight to SK. I'd been told that one of our staff, Brother Timothy, has died and find that he has not been embalmed so was bleeding from the nose, and the cardboard coffin is in a state. It really is best to let the undertakers do everything. I feel so sad.

14 September 1993. Lucille, 55, who cleaned our house for five years was diagnosed with cancer recently, so had to leave. Tom her husband phoned at 6pm to tell me she is dying so I anointed her at home at 9pm. Lots of tears, and Tom, a retired lorry driver, is distraught. They are two really lovely East Enders.

15 September 1993. Lucille died at 12.10 and I dash round to find Tom lying on the bed cuddling her, 'I loved my Lucy.' I stay for two hours with him but am worried at the amount he is drinking. They were married 35 years. I help with funeral arrangements, and Tom says, 'Tell that Robert to follow, he's a lovely man, like you. People talk about...' Then the whisky took over.

22 September 1993. Lucille's funeral which I take, I can hardly say the prayers.

28 September 1993. The first letter I open before breakfast:

Dear Malcolm, I now it is a sin against god to take your own life but I can not help it Malcolm. I begged god to take my life and let my Lucille live but he turned me down. I love my Lucille so much Malcolm I think about her and Cry daily for her I can't bear to live with out her any longer. If I am allowed a church service I would like you to do the service for me. Would you explain to the people in the church why I did it. T. Collins.

Soon after his daughter rang to tell me that he had died from an overdose of pills and alcohol.

7 November 1993. For several years I have been acting as spiritual director to a priest now 86 who today revealed a very disturbing story, but I have been given permission to tell it after his death.[99] When he was a student at Lincoln Theological College in 1932 he made his confession to Michael Ramsey who, although only three years older, was sub-warden. In the confession he mentioned that he had sex in public lavatories as this was the only place to meet people. Michael was in a dilemma but asked if he might tell the Principal, Leslie Owen,[100] which was agreed. Both men said that the orientation was a gift and he would have pastoral skills denied to others, BUT ordination must be delayed. He went to work with a charity in London and had counselling with Dr Leonard Browne of the Tavistock Clinic, a doctor and a deacon. His father, who had an old-fashioned horror of homosexuality, had to be told and asked if he would pay the fees. He said, 'Why didn't you tell me before? Didn't you trust me? On no account tell your mother.' The man was eventually ordained but has lived a hidden life, tortured by guilt in the north of England. The Church has much to be blamed for, but I am glad that the Consultation has been a tremendous support for him, and that he has made several friends. He is pathetically grateful.

11 November 1993. Today I met a most impressive human being. Jay Walmsley is a transsexual who works as a man in a

high-up position in a large international company, and she wants me to be her spiritual director which is a challenge because my knowledge of transsexualism is sketchy. However, like all spiritual direction it will be a two-way process and I shall learn a lot. As John she married in 1967 and has two daughters. The wife died five years ago, and John began to face up to the fact that since the age of seven he has felt himself to be a woman but has to do all the male things. No one at work knows the situation, but he attends a church in Caterham as a woman and most of the congregation accept her. She supports other transsexuals and is a good counsellor. She has a good doctor so my job will be to help her think theologically about the fact that her psychological gender – that indefinable feeling of maleness or femaleness – is opposite to her anatomical sex.

22 November 1993. Snow covers the City of London Cemetery as I inter Lucille and Tom's ashes. Their daughter Sheri is due to have a baby in 3 days.

2 December 1993. 'Mr Ali Khan sends his love to you,' I tell the Queen Mum. I'm sitting next to her with Lady Elizabeth Basset on the other side, at luncheon (certainly not lunch) at Clarence House, and other guests at the circular table are Lady Mary Soames, the Ambassador in Paris and John Bowes-Lyon her nephew. 'How kind,' she says, 'who is he?' Well, I was waiting for a train on Limehouse station when this young Asian spoke to me and asked where I was going so I told him. 'How perfectly charming; East Enders are so loyal.' She talked a great deal to me about SK ('It is mine, you know, Queens have always been in charge since 1147') and homelessness. She is well briefed and certainly has all her marbles. I told her that I was born in Norfolk and had some of Edward Seago's paintings. 'He used to take the King and I out in his boat; I love his paintings, a very quiet man.' I did not tell her that her chef had told me that she and Ted Seago used to walk on the beach near Overstrand and once she suggested that he swim. 'No bathing costume!' 'I'll look the other

way.' When he returned naked he found her asleep in the sun. We also look at the John Singer Sargent charcoal portrait of her – 'Drawn on my engagement.' She had been to the Smithfield Show the day before where one of her bulls won first prize and had been bought by Safeway for slaughter. She asked if it might be put to stud instead and they agreed, which greatly pleased her. Lunch was lobster mousse and white wine, chicken stuffed with mushrooms (with claret!), meringue pudding then cheese and port. A small jewelled bell summons the two footmen in scarlet tailcoats. Afterwards we went into the Drawing Room where she showed me Sickert's portrait of George V with his anxious looking racing manager. 'Almost for sure the race has been lost.' She shows Mary Soames a bronze maquette of her parents Winston and Clemmie. I left at 3pm and particularly remember her telling me that the Church needs more laughter so I should go ahead with a plan for a clergy revue in aid of charity. I will.

Christmas 1993. I have taken so many funerals of young men with AIDS and now the deaths of Lucille and Tom have pulled me down, but the Christmas cards for once have thoughtful messages:

To us, Lord
In the ice flash and the frost fall
Show yourself…
Still swaddled Saviour
Tilt our world towards springtime.
From 'Epiphany', Kevin Nicholls
Spinks and ouzels sing sublimely
'We too have a saviour born,'
White blossoms burst untimely
On the blest Mosaic thorn.
God, all-bounteous, all creative,
Whom no ills from good dissuade,

Is incarnate, and a native
Of the very world he made.
Christopher Smart

5 January 1994. Gilbert and George, the artists who gleefully shock everyone with works on religion, sex, scatology and all taboo subjects, were sitting in the front pew at Simon Pettet's funeral in Christ Church Spitalfields. I have enjoyed visiting Simon, a gifted 27 year old ceramicist, in his ground floor panelled rooms in one of the splendidly un-restored early 18th century houses – 27 Fournier Street. With coal fires and candles on wall sconces it was very atmospheric, and had been a doctor's surgery in its early years. Simon specialised in Delft blue and white tiles, tulip vases and obelisks. For ten years he had not seen his strict Methodist parents but when he was dying asked them to visit weekly. I mourned this vivacious, optimistic and good-looking man and had to take the service and do the eulogy as everyone else was so upset. In the vestry before the service the vicar, my old adversary Eddie Stride's successor, could see how upset I was so put his hand on my shoulder, 'Give Malcolm strength, Lord.' At the crematorium we played *Time to Sleep*, one of the *Four Last Songs* by Strauss.

15 April 1994. I owe Patrick Welch a great deal because his unpublished PhD thesis on Bishop Blomfield is helping me with a possible book, and I saw Patrick a lot when I was writing my MA on the Bishop. Today I was at the Golden Wedding lunch for him and Joy. During his speech he said, 'It is a great honour having the Revd Malcolm Johnson sitting next to Joy. He is Professor of English Literature at Westfield College London and in 1938 chaired a meeting at which Trevelyan spoke. It was the day I met Joy.' I got some very odd looks. I was two at the time.

26 April 1994. The ordination to the priesthood services for women have been terrific, even at St Paul's. There I was accused of being liturgically promiscuous because I laid hands on seven

women. They were each allowed to ask only five priests so I feel honoured. At Southwark I went to two services on the same day and it was immensely moving seeing old Elsie Chamberlain entering supported by two young women, and at Coventry I was one of three laying hands on Nerissa. In her study afterwards I knelt and asked for a blessing. I love her!

27 April 1994. 'Run for it, Vicar.' This was the advice from a woman passenger on the Docklands Railway when the conductor found that I did not have a ticket just as the train arrived at Shadwell station. He let me off, which he should not have done.

7 May 1994. Fair, young and handsome Rupert Haselden knows that he will die soon. We meet regularly and today he asks me about his funeral. He agrees to phone his local vicar to ask if I might officiate, but he gets a curate because there is an interregnum. She asks, 'Whose funeral?' 'Mine.' She says she must consult the churchwardens and when he rings again she says that she is sorry but she is not feeling well. 'Nor am I,' says Rupert. We give up, and I phone Sheila Cunliffe at Clapham and fix it all in her church. His partner Nigel Finch tells him that he should hurry up and die as Malcolm goes to Spain on 22nd. Today we sit on his bed to hear his plans – 'I shall speak and no one is to interrupt.' He has been a great influence in my life because he has showed me how to die: 'My bags are packed and I am waiting for the taxi to arrive.' Over the last eight months he and his mother have had counselling to heal the wounds they have inflicted on each other.

8 May 1994. When I spoke at the Ipswich diocesan conference I met a man who used to be Benjamin Britten's secretary. He said that music to Britten came before Peter Pears or anyone, or anything else, and that when his wife went into hospital Britten told him, 'You can now give me your undivided attention.'

9 May 1994. Rupert died 36 hours after I left him, but woke in the night and said, 'Have I died yet?' I feel so very, very sad.

10 May 1994. Our friend John Gladwin is consecrated a bishop (of Guildford) in St Paul's today, and I gave June Osborne the delicious story of Montgomery Campbell which she uses in her sermon. Commenting on the appointment to Guildford of George Reindorp in 1961 he said, 'The first bishop of Guildford went out of his mind, the second had no mind to go out of, then they had me, then a saint and now they have started all over again.' There are many Montgomery Campbell stories including that of his enthronement in St Paul's in 1956. He banged on the West Door three times with his crosier and nothing happened so turning to his chaplain he said, 'We've come to the wrong place.' When the doors opened to reveal the old canons he commented, 'The See gives up its dead.' When Mervyn Stockwood was appointed Bishop of Southwark in 1959 Montgomery Campbell told everyone, 'I'm taking steps to have the Thames widened,' and later when Mervyn arrived at a bishops' meeting in purple cloak, purple cassock, cincture and socks, he said, 'Hello, Mervyn, incognito, I see.'

21 June 1994. The 25th anniversary of Robert and I being together. We have two large dinner parties, straight and gay. We never think that people can let hair down at mixed gatherings. Paul Richens and his three ladies do the catering.

23 June 1994. A party is held today to launch my book on St Botolph's, *Outside the Gate*. Fortunately we could keep the price down to £9 because before I left I asked local firms to sponsor it and £4,500 was donated. My good friends Jenny Smith and Denise Jones of Stepney Books decided to print 1,500 copies and all profits will go to the crypt work. I enjoyed writing it because I had a 1,000-year canvas to cover although much space is given to the events of the last 20 years. People say it is well written and witty, and one reviewer travelled two stops further on the underground than he wanted to because it was so engrossing. There are many amusing stories like Mr Smalcole, the beadle, who was dismissed in 1786 having been caught in Holy Trinity Minories

crypt sawing up coffins for firewood or to make floorboards for his house, and Dr Fly who was incumbent for 63 years whilst also being vicar of Willesden.

7 July 1994. As commanded, I have jollied up St Katharine's chapel and today the Queen Mum comes for the dedication by Bishop David Hope of two large banners by Thetis Blacker and the sculpture *Genesis* by Naomi Blake. The banners *De Profundis ad paradisum* are stunning. They are not only decorative but will be visual aids for the resurrection – Christ the *Ichthus*, bringing us little fish, small fry, to our eternal hope, and Christ the Phoenix bringing us little birds to eternity. They will be great for our many funerals. I take the QM to see them before the service and she admires them and tells Thetis so. Her lady-in-waiting whispered to me, 'She can't see a thing.' Thetis was angry that the person who had hung them had creased them, and complained to the Bishop who fled to the vestry. Robert said that they looked OK. 'Then you have lost your critical faculties,' said Thetis. Kathleen Raine has especially written 'Water':

> But in mid-ocean of desire
> The King of Fishes stands
> Upon the teeming seas, and to him rise
> Like salmon to the poacher's light
> Miraculous drafts of Venus spawn
> As from her element we are drawn,
> From living waters into birth.

As we walk into my study the QM says that it is marvellous how I have brought so many people into St Katharine's, and that I am opening it up to the local community. 'People must enjoy being in this room talking to you about their troubles.' I suspect that she has been briefed by dear Elizabeth Basset, one of her ladies-in-waiting. It is a great affirmation, one of the greatest of my life.

1 August 1994. The Two Johns usually stay with us during the

summer and today took us to see Judi Dench in *The Seagull* at the National. As John Hencher had worked with her we went backstage and she opened a bottle of champagne. What a star; she is giggly and fun. We have several dinner parties during their visit and John H does not need much encouragement to do his party piece – we all have to join in *Sing a Song of Sixpence* doing all the actions. Middle-aged and elderly clerics making fools of themselves in our drawing room.

27 August 1994. The *Financial Times* has a piece by Michael Thompson-Noel on holidays from Hell. 'I felt trapped and concussed. There was seediness and desperation almost everywhere. I was in Great Yarmouth... which sits like a boil on England's eastern cheek. It plays host to the poorest and least sophisticated of Britain's stay-at-home holidaymakers. It gives them food to feed a pig on and a wind from the Urals.' To think that when I was a teenager I pondered whether to stay in here and work in the family firm. I had a narrow escape.

25 September 1994. Michael Turnbull, Bishop Designate of Durham, is on the front page of the *News of the World* because in 1968 he was arrested and found guilty of having sex in a lavatory with a farmer. Three archbishops, Coggan, Carey and Runcie, say that he is forgiven so it must be so. They all knew about it. So our Church condemns gay clergy with loving partners and forgives blowjobs in lavatories. It is ironic because Michael, whom I have known since university, took a very hard line on homosexuality when I asked him to lunch at the Athenaeum.

5 October 1994. David Hope and the authorities have decided that the diocesan drop-in centres for the elderly and the hostels for single mothers are in danger of losing money so they will be transferred from the Diocesan Board of Social Responsibility to a new charity, RADICLE, which I am to chair. I feel this is a great mistake because although our office will be in Diocesan House we shall no longer be a church charity. Fortunately Caroline Chartres, whom I adore, will become our patron and we have a

splendid board of trustees including John Garnett and Sue Pettigrew.[101]

2 November 1994. We are hoping that lay people will join the St Katharine's community and Dorothy Howell-Thomas has arrived. She was Archbishop William Temple's secretary during the war, and tells me that he had no chaplain and a very small staff so had to write all his speeches and sermons himself, which must have been a terrible strain and may have contributed to his early death in 1944. The Church would have been a very different one had he lived.

I went to Desmond Tutu's book launch today, and he said that when he reaches the Pearly Gates he will be sent to Hell, but two weeks later the Devil will be at the Pearly Gates asking St Peter for sanctuary.

10 November 1994. As we went into Church House for the General Synod we were met by Peter Tatchell and friends bearing placards outing ten bishops including Mervyn Stockwood, Michael Turnbull, John Neill, Brian Masters and John Klyberg. They were named because of their homophobia and hypocrisy, and I certainly feel that they have not helped the gay cause one iota. David Hope was the only one to reply, saying his sexuality is a 'grey area'.

Boxing Day 1994. At our dinner party Fr Bernard Lynch tells a story of a volunteer training day in the early years of Lighthouse, the HIV centre and hospital. The Director had been talking about safe sex and had listed all the things gay men do together. At the end a nun aged 82 put up her hand and in her Irish accent said, 'Mr Spence, would you tell us more about the f*** f*****g?'

14 January 1995. Allan died in Miami last year and his partner Bob has brought the ashes to be scattered at Ely Cathedral, one of his most favourite places. I debate whether to ask the Dean for permission, but it will make a lot of administrative chaos, so after prayers in the Cathedral we go to the Cloister Garth and scatter

them. Allan and Bob were staying with us just before Allan died, and after the funeral Bob wrote to me:

> *None of the aphorisms the Church offered me worked, and in the face of an all-consuming grief and loss, they missed the mark – the power of death to inspire a profound and 'awe-full' change in an individual and which has the potential to dismantle the very framework of the lives of those who survive. I changed or perhaps grew in ways that were totally unexpected. I saw Christ's suffering and death in Allan's suffering and death. They were one and the same. I died as well that early morning, the same time as Allan died. When I shall die I shall not be afraid, but armed with some foreknowledge, will see it for what it is.*

3 February 1995. Nigel Finch, TV producer of *Arena*, a filmmaker of startling originality, and Rupert's lover, is dying. I asked him if he would like to be anointed and explained it was oiling the wheels for his final journey, then told him that the Queen was anointed at her Coronation for strengthening. 'If it's good enough for her, it's good enough for me.'

4 February 1995. I anoint Nigel with his sister and eight closest friends kneeling round the bedside whilst the radio plays *The Good, the Bad and the Ugly* – no one thought to turn it off. I went from there to Guys to anoint David Curry who has been a friend for years and was a counsellor at the Richmond Fellowship. He died seven hours later.

10 February 1995. David Curry's funeral at St Katharine's. His sister, an evangelical Christian, is distraught not only at his death but at finding some explicit porn in his flat. I try to explain with no success, so will ask Nerissa to visit her in Birmingham. During her years at St Botolph's Nerissa and her husband David[102] were never fazed by anything.

25 February 1995. Lionel Blue on BBC 4's *Thought for the Day* spoke of our retreat with 'dimple wimpled nuns' for people

affected by the virus, and as always combined deep spirituality with humour. He tells the story of a widow left £100,000 by her husband who said, 'I'd willingly give £1,000 to have him back.'

26 February 1995. Esther de Waal, whom I knew when she was a neighbour in Tredegar Square, writes:

> *Let us live with uncertainty*
> *As with a friend.*
> *To feel certain*
> *Means feeling secure.*
> *To feel safe is unreal,*
> *A delusion of self.*
> *Knowing we do not know*
> *Is the only certainty*
> *Letting the self be lost into Christ.*

I find that immensely helpful because my faith is ebbing away. The nuns of our community are unsupportive and are always criticising and pulling me down, so I do not want to pray with them, and all these deaths of young men have hurt me terribly. I now know what the chaplains in the First World War experienced. At Nigel's funeral, crammed with his young friends and many media people including Alan Yentob and Janet Street-Porter, I quoted Edmund White – 'When AIDS arrives you have to decide whether to drop everything and look the disease in the eye, or go on with a new consecration.' Nigel did the latter.

15 April 1995. Reflecting on my experiences of what someone has called 'the gay Hiroshima' I often wonder if HIV has changed the way people look at gay men. Some will have had their prejudice that we are dirty and diseased reinforced, but some may have been impressed at how this terrible disease has been surrounded by loving care and support. Up till now I suspect many agree with a possibly apocryphal remark made by David Hope that his gay priests spend too much time, 'tarting up their

houses.' Freed from child rearing, we used to be told that we are narcissistic and focus on our bodies, clothes and careers. However, over the last ten years we have seen self-help groups created, a hospital opened,[103] bands of volunteer buddies formed and an outpouring of love which has surrounded sufferers.

21 April 1995. When I last saw Lady Elizabeth Basset I talked to her about my work with men affected by HIV/AIDS, and today she asked me to tea to show her the prayers I use. It may have been naughty but I use the opportunity to tell her of the unhappiness at St Katharine's, hoping she might tell the Queen Mum. Not all the Court of Governors are hostile. Lord Holderness, the son of Lord Halifax and a close relative of Nerissa, always treats me kindly. On court days I meet him at the back door so that he doesn't have to climb steps. In the war he had both legs blown off in Tunisia in 1943. With amazing courage he became a Conservative MP then a Minister. He went to the House of Lords in 1979, and Nerissa lobbied him to support the ordination of women.[104] I like him.

23 April 1995. I went to Tom and Doris' wedding in Havant. They have been calling the banns for 32 years mainly because Tom, a real East End priest, is gay and for years had an affair with a local dustman. Now that he is HIV+ she will look after him. The day before the wedding he left Waterloo by train for Havant, went to sleep and ended up in Portsmouth whilst Doris was on the platform at Havant. You don't need a degree in psychiatry to see what is going on. I know that she will nurse him and love him.

24 April 1995. I am honoured today to be among the *Gay Times'* Top 200 men and women. Perhaps I deserve it because the other night at 3am two women in Stockwell who I had taken a Service of Blessing for phoned to say they were about to commit suicide, and would lock themselves in a garage and breathe the car exhaust. I contacted the police who went and broke the door down. Both apologised next morning.

29 June 1995. I have learnt so much from Jay Walmsley who will have the male to female operation after she retires. I have encouraged her to do the Southwark diocesan training course for spiritual direction as I am sure she will be a good spiritual director. She has agreed and been accepted.

6 September 1995. Bapsy, the Indian Dowager Marchioness of Winchester, has died aged 93. My Great Aunt Ethel knew her in the Bahamas when she became the Marquess' third wife in 1952 thus having a father-in-law born in 1801. Her new husband was born in 1862 and his father had sired him when he was 60. Ethel had high hopes the old boy would marry her but he didn't. Her own husband, Barney, had died leaving her a large sum of money, and she enjoyed telling me that they both had represented British Honduras at the 1937 Coronation. When she was in England I was usually bidden to see her at Claridge's for lunch. On one occasion when I was fourteen I asked her after lunch if I might buy her tea. We went to Fortnum's and much to my horror she ordered expensive cakes etc. The bill came to £1 which cleaned me out completely, and meant that I had no money to buy lead soldiers. I later complained bitterly to my father who said, 'You have learnt a lesson today. If you ask someone to a meal you pay the bill no matter how wealthy they are.' However, it was a good investment because when Ethel died in 1968 she left me £5,000 – enough to buy a flat which has meant I have never had to live in church accommodation.

28 September 1995. I enter the Goldfish Bowl today by arriving in the City of London's aldermanic robing room to don my scarlet cassock, gown, black scarf, badge etc as Sheriff's chaplain. Despite my leaving St Botolph's Sir Peter Levene[105] has asked me to be his chaplain. Frank Weston, Archdeacon of Oxford the retiring chaplain, hands me the tricorne hat which has seen better days. We process to Guildhall where Peter and Ken Ayers are sworn in, then in a huge Rolls go to Drapers' Hall for lunch. I could get to like this.

29 September 1995. Panto kit again. Church service, then to Guildhall with a break between – David Burgess, rector of St Lawrence Jewry, the Corporation's church, says, 'These boys can't survive for long without a break for champagne and smoked salmon.' Sitting on the dais I have a good view of all the aldermanic beadles and the furred and gowned masters of the livery companies. A new Lord Mayor is elected, John Chalstrey who is a surgeon. He tells us: 'Over my coat of arms is a rhino because doctors have thick hides and charge a lot.'

30 October 1995. I like Peter Levene who is shrewd, clever and kind. I asked his wife, Wendy who is very beautiful indeed, if he has bought her a tiara yet.[106] Apparently not, so off to Aspreys...

22 October 1995. I am congratulated in the *Independent* and on the front page of *The Sunday Telegraph* for coming top of the clergy poll in the London Diocese's General Synod elections. Seventy-one per cent of the clergy (531) voted and I got 75 first votes. In my manifesto I described myself as 'a gay man', and Higton told the reporter Jonathan Petre that 'it shows what a state the Church of England is in.'

1 November 1995. For fun I wrote down the names of 227 gay clergy, of which 25 are retired and 42 are non-parochial. Not all come to the Consultation and nine are heterosexually married. Six are bishops and ten NSM. Seventy-one of the 227 have a gay partner and it is interesting that of the 42 non-parochial, 19 have a partner.

11 November 1995. Lord Mayor's Day. The morning begins at 9am when we drive by car from Mansion House to Guildhall for presents to be given to the Lord Mayor and Sheriffs, then after breakfast Peter and I get in a state landau smelling of mothballs to drive back to Mansion House to watch the parade from the balcony. Around 110 floats and displays pass by with several bands playing. Then we get in the landau again and go through huge cheering crowds to the Law Courts and back. The cheering surprises me, although the aldermen all have glove puppets and

squeakers to get the children going. The Lord Mayor is in the outrageously vulgar coach and the Lady Mayoress in the Pram as the Queen calls it. She uses it for Trooping the Colour – 'It's Mother's favourite.' At the Law Courts we process upstairs to stand before Lord Chief Justice Taylor, the Master of the Rolls and another judge. In front and below them is a character also bewigged but with a black cap on. Are we to be executed? Mr Justice Mellifluous, the City Recorder, tells them what a splendid chap Chalstrey is, then after he is sworn in the judges get an invite to the Banquet. We have more champagne and smoked salmon in the corridor outside, then back along the Embankment to Mansion House for lunch. It's been hard work today.

28 November 1995. In the General Synod I spoke in the church music debate on GCM – not, as I tell members, the Gay Christian Movement but the Guild of Church Musicians led by my friend John Ewington. My amendment to give the Guild recognised status equal to the Royal School of Church Music was defeated. Well, it would be – so many have vested interests.

30 November 1995. I speak again in the General Synod, this time attacking the wording of a motion: 'This Synod strongly reaffirms that marriage provides the proper context for sexual relationships.' So are all others improper? Without success I attempt in an amendment to change the wording. I wish that members had listened to Oliver O'Donovan's sermon at the Synod Inauguration Service in the Abbey – he said we should determine when we must speak, when we need to speak, and when we should remain silent.

3 December 1995. I stood tearfully in a deserted Lincoln Cathedral in front of Bishop King's statue with his hand outstretched in blessing, asking that I might be a better priest. The original design had a ploughboy kneeling in front of him, but someone suggested it might give the game away. My friend Simon Bailey, a 40 year old priest and writer, died last week from HIV after a great struggle, and I wonder how long I have left. He

was rector of Dinnington, South Yorkshire and continued there, supported by his parishioners, until he died.[107] 'The wounded surgeon plies the steel' (TS Eliot in 'East Coker').

Am here to talk to a conference, and Bob Hardy the Bishop, who I was at Cuddesdon with, tells me all is gloom in the Cathedral and that he is trying to get the Dean to leave.

1 January 1996. Douglas Rhymes died today aged 81. I followed in his footsteps at the General Synod and owe him a lot, although I always found a slight *frisson* between us. He never had a partner, and I think he was a little jealous that I did. He was much cleverer than me, and a great help in founding the Consultation and in preparing my first Synod speech. He had been in France soon after D-Day and as a chaplain conducted mass burials at Belsen, but I never heard him speak of it. He came out as gay after he retired although everyone already knew. Mervyn Stockwood was his patron, presumably providing that he kept quiet. Mervyn once told him that he advised his clergy never to attend the Consultation.

4 February 1996. Richard Chartres is about to move to be Bishop of London so Robert and I invite him and Caroline to dinner at 29 with Peter and Wendy Levene whom they have not met before, David and Tessa Brewer and Thetis Blacker. Paul Richens and his two ladies did a good meal, and Thetis pronounced Richard 'a good egg'. Recently a waiter at a City reception overheard Richard saying, 'Malcolm is a happy homosexual,' so rang me straightway.

6 March 1996. Colin Menzies, the director of Church House, often invites me to his top people's lunches during the Synod, and today I sat next to Edward Knapp Fisher who I always thought was a miserable old bugger (he did, however, give me a place at Cuddesdon when he was Principal), but today he told me a delicious story. Sir John Wheeler Barrow[108] the local squire at Garsington phoned him to say that the duchess due to open his church's fete had flu. Could he find a student to drag up and do

it? Someone agreed, and a Daimler was borrowed to convey her and her driver – the Principal heavily bearded and in chauffeur uniform – to Garsington. The students didn't recognise either of them. I *think* that the duchess went on to be Dean of Westminster. Knapp Fisher actually seemed human today, and I remember that when he left Cuddesdon to be Bishop of Pretoria we labelled his luggage: 'In transit, Pretoria Tuesday'. He married out there much to everyone's surprise as he had always advocated celibacy to students. Unfortunately the local paper in reporting the wedding got the photo captions wrong. Underneath the happy couple it said: 'Mr Smith leading in his filly after winning the Pretoria Chase', and under the horse and owner was written: 'The Bishop with his new wife'.

7 March 1996. Dorothy Howell-Thomas has left RFSK. I had such high hopes that she would add gravitas to our community. She seemed to have a blind spot about homosexuality and we had several talks in her cottage when I told her that work with gays and those affected by the virus had to be done. People come to me in the same way that ex-servicemen came to Fr Groser the famous Master after the War. She wouldn't agree and said, 'Couldn't the men's funerals be in their parish church, not here?' I tried to explain that they don't have a connection with their local church and I'm their priest. To my shame we parted badly; I met her in the corridor on her last day and said goodbye without shaking her hand.

22 March 1996. A good session with Jay Walmsley, and I suggest that she form a group for Christian transsexuals, and she is keen on the idea. They could have weekends at St Katharine's, which would be a safe place for them to meet. I was thinking that the shape of the weekend could be similar to the ones we put on for those affected by HIV – talks, meals, prayers and a party on Saturday evening with members doing their party pieces. Mine is Alan Bennett's sermon, 'My brother Esau is an hairy man but I, I am a smooth man.'

23 March 1996. Tom Wakefield, the writer, one of our closest and most dear friends, has died of hepatitis C. R and I went to the Whittington Hospital to say goodbye yesterday to be told he would not emerge from a coma. The young Chinese doctor asked if a life support machine should be used, and I took it on myself to say no, so he slipped away shortly after we left. Only 51, he had been a head teacher in a disabled children's school then a famous novelist. He loved mixing his friends together –authors like Francis King, Patrick Gale, Michael Carson, David Shenton the cartoonist, a sexy local boxer and us. He hated bigotry and believed in choosing a family instead of enduring a biological one, but as he only had a niece that was easy. Beryl his cat, 'a tabby, recalcitrant queen', lived with him in Finsbury Park and blandly watched Tom's cheerfully promiscuous life which included an affair with the local fishmonger who rejoiced in a name like Heteropoulos. When his back was painful he made Mr H stand on a table so that he could 'help' him. We adored him and he dedicated *Ten Commandments* to me, and my copy of *Forties' Child* is inscribed: 'For Malcolm who is part of my past, present and future, thank God'. With a wheezy laugh his conversation was all fizz and fun.

26 March 1996. I concelebrate at David Randall's funeral in Holy Innocents, Hammersmith which is not big enough for the huge congregation. People were standing everywhere. At the end I had to take Dorothy, his mother, to the coffin to sprinkle it. She has been a magnificent mother to him, and is one of the few saints I know. He was passionate about everything – sex, faith, priesthood etc, and I felt totally distressed today. He battled with HIV/AIDS and turned a negative into a positive by founding CARA, and counselling many men and women. It was a privilege to be one of his three-person pastoral team.[109]

2 April 1996. Today my world collapsed. Richard Chartres' secretary phoned yesterday to say he would like to call in at 7.30am, and I said, 'Am I going to be fired?' I was. He told me that

Lord Churchill, the chairman of the St Katharine's governors, wants me to leave, and will pay me for the next 3 years so that I can work somewhere else. I suspect that Ben Hanbury is also to blame. Richard said, 'I'm so sorry; I'll make sure that you are OK.' After the Bishop had gone I broke down. Why didn't Churchill tell me himself? I immediately phoned my lawyer John Underwood who thought that Robert had died because I was so tearful. When I saw him later in the day he said he would get the very best deal possible, and I should realise that it would free me from the Fawlty Towers administration of St Katharine's, and give me more time for my counselling work (I now see 50 people regularly for spiritual direction) and HIV work. No reasons were given except that they now need a live-in Master. Viscount Churchill has consistently vetoed people keen to be my live-in deputy, so now I know why. When I went to the Royal Foundation I thought that the three friars and four nuns and I could make a community. I was wrong. The sisters, except for Iona, were unhappy and I suspect jealous that all the pastoral work was done by me and the friars. George Timms, Archdeacon of Hackney, had told me 12 years ago that the sisters had made no impact recently on the local area, and I was outraged, so on 18 July 1984 I had arranged a farewell service and party for them when they moved to Vauxhall.[110] It now seems that he might have been right. In the 1950s and 1960s they were much-loved midwives in Poplar.[111]

4 April 1996. Tom Wakefield's funeral. The betting shop will see him no more! The local community adored him and turned out in force to carry his coffin through the streets to the church led by Rabbi Lionel Blue and myself. Stephen Coles takes the service. Then to Highgate for burial, and after I had said the Committal we stood and sang songs whilst the gravedigger filled the grave with earth. Tom is now lying almost next to Marx, whose bust reads: 'Philosophers have only interpreted the world... the point is however to change it'. In her poem 'New

Highgate Cemetery' in memory of Tom, UA Fanthorpe writes:

Maundy Thursday. The glamorous vicar, stripped
To a showy scarlet cassock, circulates
After the burial. Embraces shoulders,
Rubs his face against other wet faces. Borrows a hanky.

She says that Tom's heart gave out – as we might have expected. It was 'used too much for loving whoever, whatever would let him love.'

5 April 1996. Susan Howatch comes to lunch with me and I have to admit that I find her novels difficult. Susan tells me that she has been helped in her spiritual life by the books of Fr Andrew of the Society of the Divine Compassion which had a house in Plaistow. He died some time ago, and did I know that he was a painter? Yes I did, because in the boot of my car I had most of his books, and three paintings. It was a great coincidence because these had been left to me by an old lady, Janet Miller, who was born in Plaistow. She left me her belongings and I had collected them from Windsor yesterday after I had taken her funeral. I gave the books and paintings to Susan.

11 April 1996. Jay is founding a group called the Sibyls for Christian transsexuals.

12 April 1996. My heart has been in my boots all week and depression closes in particularly in the early morning. My dismissal has been a terrible slap in the face, so it is not surprising that when Ian Hislop came to interview me today for a TV programme I was a bit low. He asked me about the C of E, and I said that it is like an elderly maiden aunt whom you would like to strangle for most of the time, but comes up trumps at Christmas and Easter. She lives in a large house too big for her and beyond her means, and dislikes talking about sex or politics. 'Or God,' said Hislop.

28 April 1996. I have been elected to the Garrick and am very

honoured. I joined the Athenaeum in 1976 but have never found it very clubbable even though I was on the committee for three years. The committee who included Donald Coggan, a retired judge, and an MP would spend hours discussing what loo paper we should use, but pass momentous decisions in minutes.

29 April 1996. We have sold our beautiful 29 Tredegar Square and must find somewhere to live over in west London so Robert can get to Guildford for his job.

18 June 1996. Governors' Meeting at St Katharine's and Sheila the cook asks, 'Shall I poison the cakes?' Everyone I know seems horrified at the way I've been treated, but it will be good to leave because the governors have never understood, affirmed or talked about my work. One of them, Alison Mayne, I thought was a friend but isn't. All the others arrive – Lord Holderness, Sir Ralph Anstruther, Dame Frances Campbell-Preston, Ben Hanbury and Richard Chartres. I pass him a note, 'Beware! The cakes have arsenic in them.' Am cold, formal, terse, and tense, and tell them that I must leave by the end of the year. Richard makes it clear to me afterwards that although he disagrees with my views ('I am conservative and traditional') he will help me and will probably get me an office at St Martin's. Nick Holtam, the rector, is very affirming and helpful. A steamroller of sadness and self-pity keeps passing over me leaving me flat and squashed.

25 August 1996. Robert, I and the cats, Vita, Meg and Olly, move to our new home in Strawberry Hill, near Twickenham. Standing in the empty hall it was like the last few minutes of *The Cherry Orchard*.

20 September 1996. Our 1930s house on the river has a splendid 200 ft garden, but someone said that our furniture is saying, 'What the fuck are we doing here?' We found a porn magazine behind the boiler in the bedroom which is a bit surprising as the man who sold us the house is a born-again Christian. He asked me if I could arrange for him to see the

Queen Mother. 'She will die soon and needs saving.'

21 September 1996. Living on the Thames has its surprises. Today we were in the garden when we spotted a rowing boat parked below the trees on the opposite bank. Something pink was going up and down, and it turned out to be a young naked couple having sex.

16 October 1996. After 34 years my friendship with Bishop Edwin Barnes might be ending. We were fellow curates in Portsea and we lived in the clergy house until he married Jane. They were immensely hospitable to me, and I loved staying at their vicarages in the Guildford diocese and later at St Stephen's House where Edwin was Principal. They helped me through my marriage break-up and they like and accept Robert. However, now that Edwin is the flying Bishop of Richborough he has been saying immensely hurtful things about women's ordination and the position of gays in the Church. We somehow agreed to disagree about the women's issue – probably by not talking about it – but his comments about gays I cannot accept. After a sharp letter from me he replies, 'Even without the scriptural evidence, it seems to me that the argument from design tells against the case for homosexual practice, which is in that respect anti-natural.' He says he accepts that my relationship and those of other gay people he knows may be holy and fulfilling because we say it is, but he cannot expect the Church to uphold new models for its followers or for society. I try to tell him that being gay is not like being left handed or having auburn hair; it affects every part of you, it IS you, so if there is no acceptance of my loving I am being totally rejected. He concedes that he might be wrong.[112]

16 November 1996. Bishop John Gladwin courageously preaches at LGCM's 20th anniversary service in Southwark Cathedral. Outside a large crowd of mainly black people scream and shout Bible texts. I thanked them for coming and asked if they realised how ridiculous they look.

21 November 1996. Fred Preston came to tea today. He was

our very able regimental padre in Cyprus and has been an incumbent in Hackney since he was inducted in 1961 by the waspish Bishop Montgomery Campbell who told him that he would do no harm and might do some good.[113] The Bishop once said, 'Tell my clergy when I'm gone to weep no tears. I'll be no deader then, than they have been for years.'

5 December 1996. I read in the paper that John Phillips, formerly Vassall, died on a bus. He was on the way to have lunch with me at his club. The funeral at Brompton Oratory was two days ago so sadly I have missed it.

11 December 1996. Although I am a governor I was kept outside the Court meeting at St Katharine's for 30 minutes and then called in. My voice was hoarse and strained, and I felt angry and depressed. Lord Churchill tells me that I must leave on January 1st not the end of February as I requested; my removal expenses are agreed, but they cannot grant me the title of Master Emeritus as it would create a precedent. Cold with fury I explained that the title would show that I had done nothing wrong. Lady Ailsa O'Brien,[114] a new governor who has not met me, is too vocal. 'You are fortunate that you have been given a prestigious appointment by the Bishop' (really? Is advisor in pastoral care prestigious?). I told her that people are asking what I have done wrong. There was a long silence. She then tells me that I have not fulfilled my management obligations (how does she know?), and Churchill says everyone was sad that the sisters left. I saw red and said that they were not easy to work with. There was another long pause. I said that I would consider my position, and if they gave me a lump sum instead of paying three years' salary into diocesan funds, I would retire immediately. I told them that they have treated me shabbily, I would like some answers about status and stipend, and then walked out. At 10pm Bishop Richard phoned me at home to say that the Queen Mum would be asked to make me Master Emeritus, and that I can stay till February. 'One thing I have learnt is not to be elliptical. You

have work to do, and I want you to stay as a priest.'

18 December 1996. Things are so impossible in Lincoln Cathedral that Bob Hardy the Bishop who was at Cuddesdon with me has decided not to worship there on Christmas Day, so in *The Times* I suggest that he temporarily moves his chair, cathedra, somewhere else, and he writes to say that he likes the idea.

29 March 1997. I have now left RFSK thank God. Today I conduct the Three Hours at St James's Piccadilly with 400 there. Six addresses. Donald Reeves, the multi-talented rector, seems pleased and takes me to tea afterwards in a classy hotel.

7 April 1997. Nice welcome from Nick Holtam at St Martin's where I have a tiny counselling room, and will probably preach once or twice a month. However, I feel very dispirited and depressed.

18 June 1997. Robert's 49th birthday. He gives me so much stability and security which has meant that I have been able to keep going over the last few months. I still feel worthless, and have no wish to be in a church now.

21 June 1997. Kevin, a young very handsome East Ender who I have been caring for, died today. I took his partner's funeral three years ago. A friend said, 'He was a fabulous fuck but I don't suppose you can say that at the funeral.' He had wasted away to almost nothing, and just before he died he told the nurse to stop washing him so much – 'I'll have the cleanest arse in London.' From the next room his sister shouted, 'It will make a change.' I shall take his funeral at St Katharine's whether Churchill likes it or not.

4 July 1997. I take a BBC cameraman with me on the Gay Pride March through London. It is terrific to be part of a 330,000 strong crowd. In my dog collar I interview several people, most of whom are far too kind about the Church.

4 July 1997. Unpleasant letter from Archbishop Carey in reply to mine saying that the House of Bishops has forbidden loving

same-sex relationships; don't they realise that these give security to clergy? He writes, 'Allow me to correct you; practising homosexuality is against the discipline of the Church of England and you and I were fully aware of this when we were both ordained in 1962.' I fire off a reply asking him not to write to me in the manner of Lang and Fisher, and regretting that he had refused to read two anonymous cries from the heart which I had sent him written by London clergy in partnerships.

6 July 1997. Flea Awareness Week. My old pal Dr John Maunder, Fellow of Wolfson College, Cambridge and a leading expert on fleas and lice, is interviewed on the radio and in the press. He used to spend Christmas with us before he married, and would bring his small friends in plastic containers, some strapped to his arm. Very disconcerting, but fortunately none escaped. He said that they would starve if left in the lab over the holiday. When he talks it makes you feel itchy. His department is sent 1,000 insects every year and he gets around 6,000 phone calls from doctors etc. 'I didn't like lice but I found they grew on me.' I suggested that he should present a TV programme: 'This is your Lice'. John tells me that a proportion of the animal kingdom is homosexual, and that there are gay fleas.

15 July 1997. A debate at York in the General Synod on the report 'Issues of Human Sexuality'. Fortunately unlike ten years ago there were no cameras and not a lot of press interest. A healthy heterosexual, Archdeacon David Gerrard, puts forward our views instead of me. For the last 10 years I have been nurturing a group of supportive Synod members only some of whom are gay, and 65 turned up on Saturday evening to discuss tactics. Today David spoke well; and Paul Oestreicher made an appeal to listen and learn, saying that he had changed his mind over the years. There are about 150 very conservative laity on the Synod and I guess most of them were amongst the 506 members present. It always seems amazing to me that most debates only attract around 300 members, whereas sex always breaks atten-

dance records. Canon Wigley put the evangelical view – 'People will leave in droves if practising gays are ordained.' Michael Vasey is immensely moving, asking for a fresh look at the Bible texts and taking a swipe at his evangelical 'friends' who had tried to 'out' him, including three bishops present. He says, 'The Church is a place of danger for gay people; that is why we are leaving in droves.' Carey put the hard line, but thanked Michael and me for our contributions. In my speech I asked why there was no chapter in the report on civil rights, and pointed out that many gay and lesbian clergy lead a hidden, dishonest life which is not spiritually healthy. I told the bishops that I thought it obscene that heterosexual married men like them condemn gays to celibacy, and then I challenged the bishops who differ from the party line to band together and speak out. The Bishop of Salisbury, David Stancliffe, bought me a large gin afterwards.

17 October 1997. There were only two of us present at the funeral of Bill Parton, 82, who had been a hall keeper at the Barber-Surgeons' Hall – they sent a wreath at my prompting. He married Vera on 15 June 1940, but after her death in 1971 he started coming to the SK Group because he wanted to explore his homosexuality. He met Desmond, also a widower, and they used to dance like 'portly-plump and gay' Mrs Fanshaw in Joyce Grenfell's song:

Stately as a galleon I sail across the floor
Doing the Military Two-step, as in the days of yore.

When he came to St Botolph's he began to wear a wig which was always askew, until I persuaded him that his bald head looked attractive. When the matron of his Abbeyfield Home, who was the other person at the funeral, and I were going through all his belongings she opened a box and let out a scream because she thought that a rat was in it. It was the wig. In his will he left me everything which actually amounted to nothing because a young man had 'borrowed' thousands from him after Desmond died, then decamped. St Bartholomew's Hospital paid for the funeral.

8 November 1997. Andrew Yip, a student who came to see me several times, has published his book on 68 male, gay Christian couples. Robert and I didn't qualify because Robert is no longer an Anglican, although Andrew found that religion was not a prime concern when the relationships began. None had a church blessing. The mean age was 43.4, two-thirds are living together, 45% have a first degree, 21% are clergy, 60% are C of E, 31% have been together 10–12 years and 8% over 20 years. Surprising to me a third are physically faithful – or say they are! The book is about a very small sector of the gay world and there is no mention of pets, old age and bereavement.

8 November 1997. A curiously cold Memorial Service for Norman Pittenger in King's Chapel, Cambridge. It didn't show the warmth (and naughtiness) of the man, but did have a reading from his hero AN Whitehead's *Dialogues* that grabbed me.

God is in the world or nowhere, creating continually in us and around us. In so far as man partakes of this creative process does he partake of the divine, of God, and that participation is his immortality, reducing the question of whether his individuality survives death of the body to the estate of irrelevancy. His true destiny as the co-creator in the universe is his dignity and his grandeur.

I recently visited Norman in his squalid lodgings and was shocked by his surroundings. He was 91 when he died, and when someone asked him about his feelings on death he said, 'Frankly, my dear, I don't care a damn.'

4 December 1997. Prince Charles is present today at a packed Memorial Service in St Martin's for John Garnett[115] who died on 14 August. He attended all the RADICLE trustees' meetings, and was an enormous help to me, overseeing our new hostel in

Stepney which we will name after him. He visited it every day when it was being converted from a vicarage, and caused much merriment by telling the decorator, 'I want the front door Leander pink,' then drove away. I had to explain to a baffled painter what that meant.

9 January 1998. I feel very honoured. A gent with a superb moniker is shaking with rage at my letter published in *The Times* yesterday. 'If ever there was a more tasteless and dishonest letter written to *The Times* I do not remember it.' The Very Revd Oliver Twisleton-Wykeham-Fiennes has taken exception to my plea that the 26 places the Church of England has in the Lords should be given to laity and clergy and not just to male, unelected bishops. I wrote, 'Recent bishops have included experts in knitting, locomotives and polar exploring which no doubt was useful when these subjects were debated, but now we need to draw up a careful description of what the Upper House expects... godliness, good learning, prophetic and pastoral zeal and a knowledge of modern British culture.' Part of the fun of a letter in *The Times* (and I get about six a year published) is the abuse from respondents.[116]

30 January 1998. Lunch at the Garrick with Bruce Kinsey, chaplain of Downing College, Cambridge, who makes the point that people with a very low self-esteem get ordained because they think that they will get status and affirmation. Then they find that they belong to an institution which specialises in making them feel guilty and worthless.

6 February 1998. Having invited John Gladwin to lunch at the Garrick I waited in vain, and then at 2pm sat at the centre table. I later discovered that he jumped into a cab at Church House and spent the journey writing a speech. He was deposited on to the pavement in Soho so he paid the fare and the taxi sped away. He was standing fingering his Episcopal cross outside the Gayrock Strip Club.

8 May 1998. I drove to Jay's house to anoint her before the

operation. Am feeling apprehensive as she is so special.

24 May 1998. I preside and preach at the annual Pearly Kings and Queens Service at St Martin's. They process down the aisle, the kings in suits smothered with pearl buttons and the queens in huge cartwheel hats with dyed ostrich feathers. One garment could have as many as 30,000 buttons. They look magnificent and do much charity work, giving the money they collect to organisations like the St Martin's project for the homeless. Their founder, Henry Croft, was born in 1862 and brought up in an orphanage. He became a road sweeper and rat catcher so spent much time in the markets with the costermongers, and after a while persuaded them to wear suits covered in mother-of-pearl buttons and beads which were cheap to buy. The charity work had begun, and when he died in 1930 there were 400 kings and queens in full regalia following the hearse in their decorated carts.[117]

5 June 1998. Jay's op was a great success thanks to two skilled surgeons. A brave woman, she has a new life ahead of her.

12 June 1998. Richard Chartres has nominated me as a member of a research group at St Luke's Hospital and members include Mark Santer[118] and Michael Ball. They want to raise £1½m to study stress among the clergy. I said if they invited 200 clergy to a really good drinks party they would soon discover what the stresses are, and it would be cheaper. I raised the gay issue and pointed to research by Ben Fletcher published recently. No one seemed interested. The project will soon peter out.[119]

28 June 1998. I was working in the garden of our new house in Strawberry Hill when I was summoned to the telephone to be told that Michael Vasey has died after two massive heart attacks.[120] He was only 53, and I sat by the river alone and wept. Apparently he wanted me to be told that he was in hospital. He had signed his book *Strangers and Friends* 'with great respect' and I will miss him. The book has helped his fellow evangelicals to open their eyes. It is a terrible loss for the gay movement mainly

because he was not a one-issue person but a biblical and liturgical scholar.

16 July 1998. A young priest, who I have looked after for many years, has returned to England having spent 22 months in a Romanian prison for having sex in a park with a 14 year old boy. Whilst he was away his bishop unfrocked him, and put all his furniture and belongings from the vicarage in store. Today I went with him to see John Perry, Bishop of Chelmsford. When we arrived the Bishop said he wanted to see him alone, and we both said this was unethical. After a while we went into the study and not once did Perry ask how he was despite the man having lost two stone. The priest has always maintained that he was stitched up by the police, and that he thought the boy was much older than 14. I have never thought he was a paedophile, and said so, also asking why the Bishop unfrocked him without interviewing him. Perry said if this was to be discussed he needed his registrar present. He would not give any money to help him, but would pay for counselling. I was appalled, and will get the Synod to add a paragraph in their forthcoming debate on clergy discipline so that men found guilty abroad cannot be unfrocked until they are given a hearing on their return. We left quickly in case Perry prayed over us.

22 July 1998. The Lambeth Conference is being held with hundreds of bishops and their wives from all over the world descending on Canterbury then touring the country – the Lambeth Walk. Is it worth the huge expense and does anyone care what they think? I drove to Canterbury, and at the time of the cathedral Sunday service celebrated communion in a Methodist hall for a small group called AGLO – Action for Gay and Lesbian Ordination, and Tim their convenor thanked me and called me 'our Pink Bishop with wonderful gentleness and spiritual warmth.'

1 August 1998. We are trying to sell our Strawberry Hill house and possible buyers ask how we are related. *Partner* sounds too

business-like, *meaningful associate* too American, *chum* smacks of Biggles, *mate* a building site, *companion* is an Edwardian lady and *consort* too royal. Perhaps *Other Half* is best. One lady seeing me working in the garden in the pouring rain asked, 'Will he stay?'

11 August 1998. The bishops at Lambeth are discussing sexuality, and one of the African bishops likens us to paedophiles or those who like sex with animals. I first heard that from a lady worker of Spitalfields parish in 1970. Peter Selby, Bishop of Worcester phones me to apologise, and says he will arrange a meeting of gay clergy so they can rant and rage.

10 September 1998. I drove to Barnes to the New Grafton Gallery whose exhibition of Edmund Fairfax-Lucy opens today. I had seen a very beautiful 'Interior, Altringham Park. Bust of Canova' on the catalogue cover so arrive at 9am to find someone standing in the doorway. A notice said: 'No purchases before 10am'. Fortunately it was third on his list, so he let me have it.

23 September 1998. Brian Masters, Bishop of Edmonton died today. I have known him since he was a curate in Stepney and never cared for him. Known as Mildred, he loved his white gloves, lace and jewelled mitre, but was a closeted coward and no help to the gay cause – he didn't sign the bishops' letter disowning the Lambeth sexuality debate. He filled his Area with clones who dislike women, and I had to help some of the women there to move to another Area. When asked how he got on at Lambeth with the woman bishop of Edmonton, Canada, he said, 'I always get on with the laity.' I could never take him seriously.

1 October 1998. Robert and I move to Mill Eyot in Shepperton, an 1860s house with superb main rooms and a garden stretching down to a creek of the Thames. Swans, coots, geese, ducks are everywhere. Our cats Meg and Olly also move in but sadly Vita died a few days ago so we buried her in the garden singing, *All Creatures of Our God and King*, which surprised the workmen restoring the house for us. Our next-door neighbour, John Hanson the famous singer, died a few weeks ago but his widow

has given us CDs of his songs, so we sing along with him as we unpack.

9 October 1998. Sally Dick, a formidable neighbour, pays us a visit and quite out of the blue says, 'You'll be happy here, there are lots of homosexuals in the village.'

13 November 1998. Splendid Mansion House lunch, then as Peter Levene's chaplain I drove with him to Guildhall where in the Silent Ceremony he is 'elected' Lord Mayor. Back to Guildhall, then he and Wendy walk to Bevis Marks Synagogue near St Botolph's for a service. Walking is part of a deal he has made because he will ride in the coach tomorrow. Doing that on the Sabbath is usually forbidden. Richard Chartres comes and I have to ask him gently not to wear a pectoral cross, but one of the silver dinner plates given to him by the Orthodox Church. I know the synagogue and some of its worshippers because I go there to the Day of Atonement service every year. Built in 1700, it is a Portuguese/Spanish orthodox synagogue with the women in the gallery, and the top-hatted men downstairs. Seven huge Dutch brass chandeliers with six or eight sconces hang above us, and the atmosphere of this oldest synagogue in England is awesome. Obviously I have to cover my head so wear my tricorne hat, which an elderly gent takes a fancy to and offers to swap it for his silk topper.

Saturday 14 November 1998. Lord Mayor's Day. At 9am I glide by Rolls to Guildhall with Peter and his sheriffs, Gavyn Arthur and Brian Harris, so they can receive gifts in the Undercroft from livery companies etc. A silver mouse for Peter's computer is one of his gifts. Kedgeree, then we climb into the State Coach, an outrageous pantomime vehicle made presumably for Baron Hardup, and go first to watch the parade from the Mansion House balcony then on to the Law Courts. (We had a rehearsal at 6am last Tuesday in torrential rain. No one around except a cleaning lady at a bus stop, so we all leaned out of the gold window and waved at her. She looked as though she always saw a gold coach go by at 6am, but gave a little wave back.) Today on the way we stopped at St Paul's not for light refreshments but to hear the choir sing. No blessing as Peter is Jewish. In the coach I sit next to Peter and opposite us are the Swordbearer, Mark Carnegie-Brown, a tall patrician figure wearing a fetching fur hat, and the black-gowned and wigged Tommy Tucker, a red-faced jovial Pickwick holding the huge silver mace. My scarlet cassock makes me look more important than I am, so I graciously wave a white gloved hand to the crowd. At the Law Courts we process upstairs into the main court as though to pay a parking fine, but the full-bottomed wigged Lord Chief Justice in scarlet, ermine and black silk welcomes Peter and tells the story of a Lord Mayor who was accidentally shot by his gamekeeper. The Memorial tablet said: 'Sir Joshua Whatnot accidentally killed 12 June 1780. Well done thou good and faithful servant'. Where do they get these stories? Champagne and smoked salmon, then we trundle back to Guildhall through huge cheering crowds for lunch, stopping on the way for a tot of rum at a naval station on the Thames.

16 November 1998. The Lord Mayor's Banquet. This is my ninth so I do know what is involved, but this year I am given a 19-page ceremonial note about what happens when, and who does what. The first grace is by my Jewish confrere Rabbi Abraham Levy accompanied by the Bevis Marks choir, and I say the second grace after dessert and Tony Blair's speech. I am doing most of the duties this coming year but the Rabbi will do some. Today proceedings begin at 4.45pm in Mansion House with endless photographs in the Salon, then after Bucks Fizz and canapés we drive to Guildhall. Just before we leave I ask if we have time for a loo stop, so Tommy hoists the mace on his shoulder and leads Abraham and me to the Sheriffs' loo. At Guildhall as the top guests arrive we stand behind Peter and Wendy, who is looking gorgeous in tiara, close-fitting blue dress with train. It was really good to see Peter embrace his two sons

and his son-in-law. King Constantine and his dishy son Nikolaos, ten judges with tweenies carrying their trains, the Speaker, Lord Chancellor and Archbishop all get fanfares as they walk to the dais. The Pikemen and Musketeers are on duty, and lead us into the old library whilst everyone else finds their dinner places. At 7.07 to Handel's *Scipio* we enter Guildhall and process around the tables to our seats. There are lots of fanfares from the State Trumpeters of the Blues and Royals at each end of the Hall. Champagne with an oriental chicken and noodle salad followed by steamed sea bass with a Sauvignon Blanc. Food is by Mosimann's who gets a cheer. Beef tournedos follow with a 1990 claret then lemon tart with Monbazillac. Coffee and port. I must look flushed because Iris asks, 'Are you wearing make-up?' I get the last train to Shepperton then a taxi. What a day.

2 December 1998. I say grace at the State Banquet for the President of Germany, who asks me what my job is, so I tell him that I try to keep Peter down to earth because everyone treats him as God.

6 December 1998. A large congregation in Guildford Cathedral for a Service for World AIDS Day, and I preach. I slip coming down the pulpit stairs and land on my backside. The verger leading me back to my stall didn't even look round.

3 February 1999. Thanks to the vicar Chris Swift I am invited to take part in the Sunday morning services at St Nicholas Shepperton. He and his wife Sandy are a splendid pair and he is a clever and good parish priest. Last Sunday an elegant tall auburn-haired woman read the lesson perfectly and I congratulated her; so many murder scripture. This morning she read again and I was thrilled. Chris whispered, 'That's the actress Carole Boyd who plays Lynda Snell in *The Archers*.'

Good Friday 1999. I preached in a packed St Paul's Cathedral at 5pm. All very solemn and gloomy with a choir of 70 in black cassocks under the dome. I had sweated over my sermon, and after it we had the magnificent *He was Crucified* by Antonio Lotti.

I received the generous fee of £12.

3 June 1999. When I visit Mother who is now in Marine Court Residential Home on the Front in Yarmouth (Bert died a year ago), I stay with Jean my much-loved aunt. Today I visited Yarmouth Cemetery and found the grave of John Johnson who is my great-great-great-grandfather. He fought at Waterloo and my cousin has the medal;[121] the gravestone is marked 'Waterloo Veteran'. He died in 1878 aged 83 and it was his son, John William, who founded the family firm.

29 June 1999. Today the Archbishop hosts one of his hospitality days (the theme is homosexuality) at Lambeth, and I am one of 30 present. I felt like a black man at an apartheid rally, and was not impressed when he began by saying that he had no intention of changing his mind. The only dishy man there was Jeremy who works to make gay men straight. I ask him why anyone would want to spend their life doing that and he replies enigmatically, 'Personal circumstances.'[122] A mother of a teenage gay son asked Dr Carey where role models could be found for him, and I said not from the clergy as we could not share our experiences. 'Come off it, Malcolm,' he says, 'everyone knows that you have a partner.'

24 July 1999. Memorial Service at Poplar for one of the few saints I have met – Daphne Jones who worked in the East End in the 1950s with Fr Joe Williamson and another saint Nora Neal among the prostitutes in Cable Street. Once she was sitting on a wall with them when a police van arrived and they were all bundled inside. At the station the sergeant asked them their job and Daphne replied, 'Social Worker.' 'Then you should be ashamed of yourself,' he told her. One of her girls used to send Valentine cards to eminent clergy like the bishop and archdeacon signed DAPHNE JONES.

2 August 1999. Monica Furlong discussing the Church of England in *The Times* compared it to a second-class golf club, so as Arthur Johnson I wrote to her saying that I am secretary of the

second-class Shepperton and Sunbury Golf Club and I resent the comparison. She hadn't realised we had moved, so sent a reply, 'I loved your letter... I am sure you are a vastly superior organisation. I apologise unreservedly!'

7 September 1999. Michael, who is typing my book on Bishop Blomfield, has a splendid typo – Instead of 'Archbishop Howley did not know how to address girls, often saying my dear female women', Michael had written *undress* for address.

2 October 1999. Nearly finished my chaplaincy duties. Quite rightly Peter gets very angry at the tedious services and long sermons in St Paul's, and tells me so on the return journey to the Mansion House. Recently Nazir-Ali of Rochester preached for 27 minutes to the United Ward clubs, and Butler of Southwark 21 minutes to 800 schoolchildren.

10 October 1999. I love preaching at St Martin-in-the-Fields because the congregation is a meeting of the United Nations, and the large numbers of regular worshippers always talk intelligently about the sermon afterwards. Today I preached on preaching, reminding the congregation of the delicious Canon Chasuble in *The Importance of Being Earnest* who only had one sermon – on the meaning of the manna in the wilderness. He tells Miss Prism, 'It can be adapted for any occasion, joyful or distressing. I have preached it at Harvest celebrations, on days of humiliation and festal days. The last time I delivered it was as a charity sermon on behalf of the Society for the Prevention of Discontent among the Upper Orders.'

2 November 1999. There is an excellent obituary in *The Times* of my friend Michael Gillingham the fine art dealer and organ expert, who died on 22 October aged only 66. The sudden death of his partner Donald Findlay last year was a devastating blow. Michael was a feisty, Trollopian character and made the best gravy (with Stilton cheese) I have ever tasted.

17 November 1999. In question time at the General Synod I ask if the C of E would be better represented in the Lords not by 26

bishops but by 2 archbishops, 8 bishops, 8 clergy and 8 laity (the last two would include women). The Archbishop's reply was that: 'The Lords Spiritual are not mandated delegates of the Church of England. In an episcopal church they are senior figures of spiritual authority who are summoned by the Queen, and who seek in Parliament as elsewhere to give voice, in accordance with their conscience, to the spiritual and ethical dimensions of our national life.' Well, he would say that, wouldn't he?

A motion is passed in the Synod today urging more men and women to join the monastic life. I ask why we should encourage people to join them because the teaching orders don't teach, the nursing orders don't nurse, and Religious seem not to know what they should be doing. (The Haggerston sisters are an exception.) Several members said that it needed saying even if it was unpopular and George Carey actually said that members 'should listen to Mr Johnson.'

4 January 2000. I wrote to *The Times* telling the editor that of the 5,483 letters he published in 1999, 230 (4.2%) were from clerics writing on theology and morality but also subjects such as bird watching, drinking fluids, men's six packs, cricket, and fees for sitting on aeroplanes with dead bodies. I had, of course, no way of knowing whether the chairman of the Ramblers Association is in holy orders, but I did rumble the chairman of the UK Xenotransplantation Interim Regulatory Authority – Lord Hapgood, the former Archbishop of York. The letter was published.

18 April 2000. A young man, whose parents had come to talk to me about him a few months ago, threw himself under a train yesterday so I have spent the afternoon with them and his brothers. He rang his father seconds before he did it, 'Goodbye, I love you.' It is so very distressing but the parents are magnificent. After our first talk I came to the conclusion that the man, only 19, was transsexual not gay and had told them so.

Good Friday 2000. Many teenagers attended the young man's

funeral in his village church yesterday; I had to preach. The coffin was carried from their nearby house with 80 people following, and afterwards it was buried in the churchyard. Heartbreaking. On the way to the grave the evangelical vicar quizzed me about homosexuality. What a moment to choose.

2 May 2000. An archdeacon in the diocese has been asking clergy the exact nature of the relationship between them and their lodgers, so I wrote to the Bishop of London who tells me he had heard this 'from several sources', and will tell the gentleman 'how much damage can be caused by such intrusive enquiries.'

1 June 2000. There was nearly a headline in the local paper – 'Vicar strangles bride's mother'. At the rehearsal she interfered and changed things constantly and today her daughter was nearly half an hour late. Later talking to Carole Boyd she hinted that Lynda Snell's strangulated ex-estuary vowels are cribbed from this woman.

27 June 2000. In the silence before grace at Guildhall, Iris Samuels leans over and shouts, 'Aren't you lucky I invited you?' Yes I am! The Queen Mum's 100th birthday is being marked by this luncheon, and we are all given a satin menu in a velvet-covered oblong box. Much champagne before, then at tables for 12 we are given lobster, lamb, Eton mess, each accompanied by superb wines. HM is given paintings by Piper and Varley. At the toast George Carey took her wine glass; Queen Elizabeth's, 'That's mine' comes over the loudspeaker. As she left on the arm of the Lord Mayor we all sang, *If You Were the Only Girl in the World*.

10 July 2000. My last time at the General Synod after 15 years listening to debates mainly on money, law and sex. Here at York University the sun shines, the ducks crap and we do at least talk to each other, unlike in London. Today we agree to initiate a study on consecrating women bishops. Voting was bishops 36–1; clergy 154–39 and laity 165–49. Where are the other 200 members?

3 October 2000. I sat in the train opposite a handsome 30 year old man with short hair, earring, bulging biceps and a T-shirt inscribed 'Thieving rich footsucker acupuncture'. He was reading *Governance of Anglo-Saxon England*. Last week I sat opposite a gorgeous young man in a brand-new dog collar. I hadn't got mine on but as we drew into Waterloo I couldn't resist telling him that I too am ordained, and asked which parish is he in. 'Oh, I'm not a priest, I'm going to a vicars and tarts party.'

18 November 2000. A memorable *Hamlet* at the National with Simon Russell Beale as the sweet Prince and Denis Quilley as Polonius. Ophelia tells her father a few home truths which apply to me as well:

Do not as some ungracious pastors do
Show me the steep and thorny way to heaven,
Whiles like a puffed and reckless libertine
Himself the primrose path of dalliance treads,
And reeks not his own rede.

Primrose Path would be a good title for this diary, but John Mortimer has used it already.

25 November 2000. Runcie says that he could not help Diana because of the Establishment. I thought that was one of the reasons for having an Established Church.

3 January 2001. The editor of *The Times* publishes my letter saying that in 2000 only 205 letters came from clerics, a drop of 0.5% on 1999. One or two people wrote to say I clearly have nothing better to do.

18 January 2001. I have never typed or used computers so am on a 10-week course at Staines: 'Gently into computers'. The tutor is very understanding as I am wildly out of my comfort zone. He started by saying, 'This is a mouse.'

25 January 2001. Queen Victoria died 100 years ago and Hibbert's new biography is splendid. I particularly liked the

story of one of her grandsons who wrote from Wellington College saying that he was broke; could he please have a sub? She replied at length saying no. Back came the reply saying that it didn't matter because he had sold her letter for 30 shillings.

10 February 2001. *The Times* obituary of Philip Goodrich, Bishop of Worcester says that he was a liberal churchman, which is news to me. He forced one of his curates to live apart from his boyfriend of three years standing, and when I wrote to complain replied, 'There are some unpleasant things a bishop has to do.'

11 March 2001. I broadcast to the nation yesterday, giving two talks in the Morning Service from St Martin's. Theme was 'hospitality' and there were many flattering comments, although John Ewington said that he queried my comment, 'You and I do not have much space to offer,' when Robert and I live in a huge Victorian house with three reception rooms and six bedrooms. It reminds me of the grace I said at a Guildhall banquet which

The Queen Mother with Lady Elizabeth Basset (left) and Naomi Blake (sculptress) at the Royal Foundation of St Katharine, July 1994.

Fulham Palace September 2001. Bishop Richard Chartres at the launch of my book *Bustling Intermeddler?*

began, 'Lord, give us a heart for simple things.' When we sat down amid the gold and glitter someone leaned over and said, 'Simple?'

27 March 2001. Funeral in Guildford Cathedral of my dear friend Roger Robins, who was one of four ordinands in my curacy years in Portsmouth. He was then 19 and I was in love with him in those days. The other three were among the robed clergy. Roger has battled with MS for the last few years. I married Roger to his first wife Elaine and after she died I married him to Chris in St Botolph's and I am godfather to his two daughters, Ann and Katie. I felt quite devastated at his death so am glad I only had to do the committal at Woking. The hearse broke down so Rog was late for his own funeral, and as we waited at the West Door I asked the other three if they realised in the early 1960s that I was in love with Rog. One replied, 'We didn't think about such things in those days.' I had helped Chris with all the

arrangements, and she was bothered that she had not put his underpants with the clothes taken to the undertakers. Did it matter? They rang to say, 'We can't have him enter the Cathedral without underpants.' I also told the undertakers that by tradition a priest enters head first which they did not know.[123] The Cathedral was full. A friendship of nearly 40 years has ended.

12 September 2001. The Wednesday Midday Service at St Martin's is usually moderately well attended, but because of yesterday's horrors in America we had well over 100 there, mainly Americans. The choir on their usual good form and I attempt to preach relevantly on 'The Mystery of Iniquity'.

20 September 2001. Fulham Palace (thanks to Richard Chartres) hosts the launch of my biography of Charles James Blomfield, Bishop of London 1828–56, who lived and died there. *Bustling Intermeddler?*[124] is published by Gracewing. Amongst the 110 guests were about 30 members of the Blomfield family and John Brooks,[125] now 92, who was the Vice Principal of Cuddesdon when I was a student there, and who encouraged me to research this neglected reformer and administrator. Howell Harris Hughes, secretary of the Church Commissioners (founded by Blomfield in the 1830s) has been a tremendous support in helping financially and meeting me for lunch regularly – he describes these meals as 'life enhancing'. Jane Ellison, Bishop Gerald's widow, who helps in the Palace library (where Blomfield died), and I laugh about all my controversial talks with Gerald. I have often pondered why I am so interested in Blomfield – perhaps because he was not frightened of unpopularity.

16 October 2001. On this day in 1635 Sir John Gayer met a lion in Africa who mercifully ignored him. Later in his life when he was Lord Mayor of London he instituted the Lion Sermon at St Katharine Cree and I gave the 358th sermon today, with some of his descendants sitting in the pews. I said that obviously the lion did not eat Sir John because either he had had lunch, or there was something better on offer. Afterwards someone wondered if Sir

John had wet himself because lions do not like human urine.

25 October 2001. I resign today from my Masonic Lodge – 313 United Friends, Great Yarmouth. It is one of the oldest Lodges in England and Nelson belonged to it. Being a mason has never bothered my conscience, and I have always thought that they take greater care of each other than do the members of the Church. When Father died they visited Mother immediately to ask if they could help. I was initiated soon after my 21st birthday in 1957 on my condition that Father bought me a new suit. As I paraded round the Lodge blindfolded with my jacket removed and trouser leg rolled up I thought that I heard a titter or two. When I got outside the Tyler told me that I had forgotten to remove the large price tag on the back of my trousers.

20 November 2001. When I went to a fellow priest's interminable retirement service a year ago I was bored out of my mind, so vowed I would have an Entertainment to mark my retirement instead of a service. In July with Nick Holtam's agreement I sent out 350 invitations asking friends to pay £10 each for food, wine and cabaret in St Martin's, and tonight we had around 500 there with 451 tickets sold so were able to send £1,734 each to Stonewall and St Martin's Social Care Unit. Lionel Blue who called me 'our bishop' provided the jokes, Michael Cashman, Roland Macleod, Roger Royle, Jamie Newall and Eric James did readings, Michael Marshall played the piano, Philip Sawyer played the violin and the Gay Men's Chorus opened and closed the show with jaunty numbers such as *Hello Dolly* and *The higher the barriers the taller I walk*, an apartheid song. In the middle of proceedings we remembered those not with us because of death, and I read the names of 40 men whose funerals I have taken, and whose relatives were there. Rabbi Mark Solomon then sang the haunting Jewish lament *El Male Rachamim* – God is full of compassion. It was heart stopping.

29 November 2001. Richard and Caroline Chartres give a black tie dinner for me at the Old Deanery and I chose the guests

– Peter and Wendy Levene, David and Tessa Brewer, Thetis Blacker, Liz Crowther[126] and, of course, Robert. It is a splendid affair and Richard talks of my Ministry Sans Frontiéres. He tells me that when he invited Ken Livingstone to lunch to meet church leaders he walked in to the room and pointing at the Cardinal said, 'What's he doing here?' He meant the painting of Henry VIII on the wall above the Cardinal's head.[127]

21 June 2002. This year I am, at the invitation of David Brewer, the Master's[128] chaplain at the Merchant Taylors' Company, and at noon today I preach to them in St Helen Bishopsgate which is extremely evangelical and was my main opponent in the City. As we processed in I passed Sir Timothy Hoare and said to him, 'I bet you didn't expect to hear me preach here,' and he grimaced. I must be doing something wrong because the new incumbent, William Taylor, congratulated me on a good gospel sermon.

28 September 2002. Chad Varah shouts at me across the drawing room of the Athenaeum, 'Malcolm, I'm ashamed of you,' and loudly berates me for my anti-hunting letter in *The Times*. He says that I of all people should not want to limit people's freedom. I tried unsuccessfully to explain that I was horrified at the cruelty of it, and ashamed that John Oliver, Bishop of Hereford, and others has said hunting is 'a legitimate recreation compatible with Christian belief.'

12/13 November 2002. Since 1997 I have been consultant to two teams of clergy in Suffolk – centred on Halesworth and Southwold. Four times every year I spend a day with each of them from 11 until 4, and stay the night at Yarmouth so I can see Mother. Both teams have huge problems ministering to a central town surrounded by 11 tiny parishes, each with a medieval church. Two churches have no electricity so someone has to pump the organ, and the one church which won't have a woman priest might fall into the sea soon. Sunday attendance varies from two to 120. The four full-time clergy in each team, who have to be careful in criticising anyone because they are probably related to half the village, could not exist without the OLMs – ordained local ministers. These are men and women of very high calibre, some retired, some not.

9 December 2002. I am given a Honorary MA by the London Metropolitan University for my work in the City and East End. Sir Peter Hall gets a Hon PhD. We have lunch together then suitably gowned I go with Robert and sit on the stage of the Barbican in front of hundreds of undergrads and their proud parents. The Lord Mayor, who is Chancellor, missed lunch and arrived at the beginning of the ceremony. I'm first up and he sings my praises and puts a hood over my head. Then he talks for a while about Sir Peter and spells out his huge contribution to the British theatre over the years. The only trouble was that this Sir Peter is an engineer who has been largely responsible for the Channel Tunnel and Hull Bridge. Whoops.

28 January 2003. Eddie Erdman has died aged 96 and I shall miss him, because after our short-term falling out over LGCM we lunched every six months at Kettner's or the Garrick, and he helped so much with our first hostel.

31 May 2003. Doris Boyd, the most famous volunteer in St Botolph's homeless centre, has died. She was recently given an MBE, and I went to see her in her tiny south London flat to say goodbye. One of my greatest supporters, she was always angry at people attacking the gay world. When I interred her ashes in the St Botolph's churchyard a drunk homeless man handed me a poem to read:

Doris we can only stand and pray
Around the ground where hense you lay
So many thoughts going on around
Remembering you without a sound
All us people you have helped many times
But we still drink are lager and limes
It must have broke you heart

To see many of us end up in Barts
But some of us are getting there

10 June 2003. I had no idea that Bill Skelton, who used to worship at St Botolph's with his partner of 21 years Chris Eldridge, had a DFC and Bar as well as a DSO and Bar. A gentle, quiet priest, he never talked about his time in the Second World War as a night hawk, becoming a famous navigator with the pilot Branse Burbridge. In his time he had turned down the bishoprics of Kingston and Liverpool probably because he found it impossible to put his faith and sexuality together. After a severe emotional breakdown in 1969 he left the full-time ministry and became director of the Lambeth Endowed Charities. It was a great honour for me to read the prayers today at his Memorial Service in Southwark Cathedral where we interred his ashes in the lawn.

20 June 2003. Graham Dow, Bishop of Carlisle seems a simple soul. He condemned the appointment of Jeffery John as Bishop of Reading because 'the penis belongs in the vagina and that this is something fundamental to the way God has made us.'[129] Much worse are the comments contained in his 1990 booklet *Explaining Deliverance*. In it he wrote that evil spirits could be introduced into the world through miscarriages, abortions, oral and anal sex. He thinks that people who repeatedly wear black or who always purchase a black car may be possessed by evil spirits. In a footnote he writes, 'There is a view that both anal and oral sexual practices are liable to allow entry to spirits.'

30 January 2004. A letter from the General Secretary tells me that I have been elected to the Society of Antiquaries of London, which is a great honour. My dear friend Peter Galloway mustered support for this and I am grateful. Pamela Tudor-Craig, Lady Wedgwood commented that I am more of an action man than an antiquary but still supported me. Its foundation dates from 1707 and its premises are in Burlington House where there is a splendid library of around 130,000 books that I shall use.

1 February 2004. I preach at Worcester College, Oxford on Jesus asking: 'Who do people say that I am?' The reply I do not quote is, 'You are the eschatological manifestation of the ground of our being, the Kerugma of which we find the ultimate meaning of our interpersonal relationships.' And Jesus said, 'What?'

13 March 2004. I am telephoned to be told that the St Botolph's homeless project has gone bust, owing £450,000. All the staff are sacked. I am stunned and very angry indeed. How could the finance committee and the auditors allow such a thing?

2 April 2004. I have calmed down a bit about the project going bankrupt, but now feel deeply distressed and depressed. My successor as rector, Brian Lee, phoned me but his explanation didn't make sense. Fortunately the four hostels will continue because the housing associations I worked with will take them back, but the crypt work has ended. It seems strange that last November there was a high profile fund-raising lunch at the Bank of England. What has happened? Eric James has written to the *Church Times* asking that the Bishop institute an enquiry.[130]

1 September 2004. After 10 years as Chair of RADICLE I'm giving up, so they have asked me to be President. The diocese asked us to leave Diocesan House three years ago, so we now have our HQ in our John Garnett House in Tower Hamlets. Despite diocesan fears we are still in business, have a healthy bank balance and have doubled the number of centres and hostels. Around 800 people, half over 80, visit our centres. John Reynolds is our very capable treasurer – he volunteered at St Bots in 1985 and is now a successful merchant banker and chair of the Church Commissioners Ethical Investment Committee. I married him to Karen and baptised their triplets.

5 September 2004. Our friends Ian and Robert have adopted two brothers, Richard and Lee, who have spent all their lives in foster homes. After many interviews Westminster Social Services agreed to the adoption, and as the boys are 5 and 6 a primary

school had to be found. The local Anglican school refused them admission despite Ian being a priest/therapist, but the Roman Catholic school accepted them and the Head said, 'It will teach our children a lot and we shall call you Daddy Ian and Daddy Robert.' Today thanks to Colin Slee, the Dean of Southwark, the boys were baptised at the main morning service in the Cathedral, and I am a godfather to both of them. They both have very fair hair so look like angels, and when they visited us I was bothered because I am not used to children; when we went to Shepperton Lock I spent most of the time worrying they would fall in. They didn't, and we had a splendid lunch; then Robert took them to Brooklands to see the cars and planes.

23 December 2004. The staff of Hanworth Crematorium are in mourning because their bereavement counsellor has died. Shelley arrived in 1986 and since has attended funerals and met and comforted many mourners. When she was seriously ill the undertakers collected £250 for her vet fees. She often curled up in a wreath near the cat-afalque and of course it is a very warm building to live in. Being a handsome tortoiseshell she had no difficulty in mixing with the families many of whom later brought her toys and titbits. I suggested that she be made an MBE, Mog of the British Empire. Sadly she was run over by a hearse.

18 April 2005. Around 100 people, including the Lord Mayor of Westminster, come to the crypt for the launch of my *St Martin-in-the-Fields* and +Richard makes a speech. In his Foreword he says that I tell the story 'with relish and reasonable discretion.' I have enjoyed writing it because I got to know so many interesting people, living and departed. Two vicars became archbishops and two went to prison, and the present incumbent, Nick Holtam, is a splendid man who is presiding over the circus with youthful enthusiasm.

2 June 2005. To the Mansion House to receive the Badge of the Order of Mercy from Sir Robert Balchin, the President. A very

grand affair – trumpeters, Lord Mayor and my friend David Brewer. Twenty-five of us are given this for 'distinguished voluntary work' – in my case setting up four hostels. I have no doubt that my dear friend Peter Galloway arranged this as he has always been so supportive. +Edmonton comes to be with me as does Robert. The first awards were given in 1899. Am very honoured by it all and enjoyed looking at the handsome ushers from the cavalry.

3 July 2005. I baptise my cousin's grandson on board HMS Cattistock in Poole Harbour – the baby's father is one of the officers. We upturn the ship's bell, fill it with water and I baptise Benjamin. My own baptism was on 27 January 1937 and I was named after Malcolm Campbell[131] who my mother worshipped from afar – he broke the world land/water speed records reaching 146 mph in his boat *Bluebird* in 1939.[132] Father wanted me named Max because it would be a good name in business, but thank God Mother won.

4 October 2005. Robert and I met Bishop Gene Robinson who is to speak at St Martin's tomorrow so I gave him my book on the church. I cannot think how he has survived all the stress, but he seems confident and relaxed. Unlike our bishops he was elected by his diocese so has the support of his clergy and laity. Giles Fraser, the vicar at Putney, has transformed the building where we meet, so it has pleasant meeting rooms with river views.

27 October 2005. I have decided to try and get a PhD at King's London using my research on the crypts and churchyards of the City and Westminster. After 45 years as a priest I have little interest in theology so I approached the History Department at King's and was interviewed by the Head of Department, Professor Arthur Burns. He holds the Chair in Modern British History and has degrees from Oxford where he was at Balliol. He has published several books and articles, and was one of the editors of the splendid *St Paul's: The Cathedral Church of London 604–2004*. He has an intellect the size of Surrey and I was sure

that he was far too important to take me on himself. He did. He is enthusiastic but reminds me that this must be a thesis not a book. Perhaps it would be easier to grow begonias in my retirement, but I will persevere.

The subject is 'Burial in the two cities of London and Westminster'. Today there are 61 former churchyards and burial places in the Square Mile and 17 in the City of Westminster. I have already visited these, but now I need to research the churches which no longer exist.

Then there are the crypts. Eighty-six City churches were lost in the Great Fire, of which 33 were not rebuilt but those that were had crypts. By 1800 eighty churches in the two cities of London and Westminster had crypts containing coffins; today there are fifty-nine.

21 December 2005. Civil Partnerships become legal today, so Robert and I go to Walton Registry Office where we say we don't want a ceremony, thanks. After 36 years it seems rather unnecessary although we have lunch afterwards with John Gaskell and Roland Macleod, our witnesses. The lady registrar asks if we would mind if her staff attend the service for training purposes and we say yes we would mind. Both of us are 'company directors' on the form as there has been a lot of press interest even in Surrey and although I am a has-been priest I am still a priest. In the evening I write to Tony Blair to thank him for this momentous move; if anyone ten or twenty years ago had told me this would happen I would have laughed in their face.

7 January 2006. Robert and I have moved from Mill Eyot because we need the cash to fund Robert's plan to develop a site in Weybridge. The Shepperton house was pure delight, but during our seven years we had only restored the first two floors and one room on the top floor, all connected by a magnificent staircase. The conservatory, opening out from the dining room, is still derelict. A top BT executive and his American wife have been asking us for two years to name a price, and now we have, so they

have their trophy house with a splendid garden running down to a creek of the Thames. We now live in an early 1930s Weybridge house which is the sort of home Richmal Crompton's William would have lived in. Dark, low ceilinged, large rooms, lattice windows, wooden doors and bells (which ring in the kitchen) to summon Ruby to come and tidy up or make a fire. During the war the local Tory MP lived here and there is an underground Anderson concrete shelter in the garden. It reminds me that during the war I slept in a Morrison shelter during air raids. On our first morning in Weybridge a woman appeared on the doorstep at 9am demanding £6. This was Cilla, a neighbour whose car had been covered in ash from our builder's bonfire. He had promised to pay for a wash. So not 'welcome' but 'cough up'. 'Are you renters?' she asks.

1 February 2006. At 6am Robert looked into the garden where there was a TV parked on the lawn with credit cards strewn around it. He phoned the police who told him not to touch anything but look to see whose name was on the cards. It was the same neighbour, so he rang her doorbell and her dishevelled husband denied they have been robbed until he finds that his new TV is missing. Another neighbour is the local vicar, Brian Prothero, who has not bothered to welcome a fellow priest to the parish.[133]

15 April 2006. I am not keen to go to Civil Partnership junketings, but today I do go by train to Bournemouth where two friends dressed in morning coats have a Beano in the Town Hall for over 100 guests. I feel decidedly uncomfortable, and decide it is because 12 years ago I took a Service of Blessing for them and this is not referred to at all. They behave as if they have never taken vows, and they have.

13 July 2006. The Archbishop of Canterbury's right to confer degrees is derived from Peter's Pence Act of 1533. The five or six given most years are not honorary degrees but are legally substantive degrees only given to men and women of learning.

Lambeth Palace, July 2006. Rowan, Archbishop of Canterbury, awarded me an MA.

So I am *very* honoured indeed that at Lambeth today Rowan gives me an MA which will carry an Oxford hood because that is his university. Before the ceremony in the chapel the seven[134] of us have a chance to talk with him and I asked how he is, to be told, 'I get up in the morning.' Then rather cheekily I ask if he would like to return to academic life after the Lambeth Conference. 'No, I'd like to have a smallholding in Wales and write poetry.' The service, led by the Southwark Cathedral choir, is very impressive with lots of Latin read fluently by Rowan. My citation mentions my work for the homeless and for those affected by AIDS/HIV.

25 November 2006. The evangelical so-called Christian Unions in the colleges have been complaining that the student unions are discriminating against them. Evangelical bishops including Cassidy and Carey sent a letter to *The Times* supporting the CUs.

Today a letter from Alan Robson redresses the balance, saying that the CU should be tolerated, but because it is the extreme end of the evangelical spectrum it is dogmatic and anti-intellectual, and its enthusiasm for the Bible does not extend to scholarly or critical study of it. With their intolerant views they can be a worrying presence although many grow out of it. When I was a chaplain at Queen Mary College I went to one of their

Robert and I. 2008. Photo by Paul Thurtle.

meetings and the Minutes the following week said, 'a number of the unsaved were present.'

27 November 2006. I sat next to Peter Sallis at the centre table in the Garrick, and he told me that he was in Gielgud's '*Richard II*' at the Lyric Hammersmith in 1954. I can still see Paul Scofield as Richard, and as it was a milestone in my theatre going I asked what part he played. Gielgud told Sallis that he had two very handsome men to play Bushey and Bagot so, as a contrast, he could play Green. In the event he was the Duke of York's servant. Another theatrical treat for me was in 1964 at the newly opened Chichester Festival Theatre with Olivier as director. Members of my youth club at St Mark's in Portsmouth would cycle over there at dawn to get cheap seats for that day's play. We saw Michael Redgrave as *Uncle Vanya* with Olivier as Astrov supported by Sybil Thorndike, Lewis Casson, Joan Plowright and Joan Greenwood. What a cast.

1 December 2006. Thetis Blacker asks me to go and see her about her funeral because she has an inoperable cancer and has refused chemotherapy. She is in a very pleasant nursing home, and when I arrive is clutching a four-page letter from Prince

Charles written in his own hand. She and her sister Carmen have been great friends of his, and I suspect that Thetis was a mother figure to him. I feel so sad but try to discuss the various options for the funeral and memorial service. Fortunately Robert and I gave her lunch on 18 September with Pat Grayburn at the Café de Paris in Guildford and had a high old time.

10 December 2006. Robert and I go to say goodbye to Thetis, and sit each side of the bed holding her hands as she asks for our strength to flow through her. Despite the drugs she is in pain and shouts that if she was an animal she would be put down – 'Why do you Christians want everyone to suffer?' I have no answer, but ask the nurse to see her as we leave.

18 December 2006. Thetis died today, and much colour and fun has gone out of our lives. She loved inviting her friends to parties and meals, and for 30 years was a friend to both of us. I have promised to do the committal after the Guildford Cathedral funeral so that everyone can meet together for tea.

10 July 2007. In 45 years I have never taken the funeral of a baby. In 1962 their tiny coffins were usually buried alongside the first coffin of the day in the cemetery, and parents were never present. Today at Woking Crematorium I preside over the service of Angel Marina only 30 weeks. Her parents who are 19 are supported by their family, and dad, a locksmith, carried the small white coffin into the chapel. I had taken advice from Sue Dauncey, who is a parish worker in Hornsey and was one of my directees who has great experience. Her helpful prayers meant that the service was beautiful, and the family said so. At the end we left the couple alone for a while and then I returned to do the committal. I had done it all in overdrive, and was OK until I got in the car when I burst into tears.

5 August 2007. Two senior lecturers at King's interview me to see if I should be upgraded and continue my PhD. I fail, and feel like throwing myself in the Thames. As Arthur Burns warned me, I have been writing a book not a thesis, so am given six months

off.

18 November 2007. Chad Varah has died, and in my *Church Times* obituary I recount a story he told me. The prebendaries of St Paul's were in their vestry when an administrator walked in and said, 'There is an important service here next week and world leaders will be present, so I hope you don't mind giving up your stalls.' There was a long silence then Chad said, 'Well, I mind,' and all the others chorused: 'So do I.' Chad always led, and others followed. When he was a curate he took the funeral of a girl who when her periods began committed suicide thinking that she had a terrible disease. Chad told me that he looked into the grave and said, 'Little girl, I promise that I will devote my life to make sure this never happens again.' He founded the Telephone Samaritans in 1953.

22 December 2007. I take funerals if no one else can be found because the ash cash comes in handy to pay my college fees. I always visit the family before the service and plan it with them. It does, of course, mean that I meet people right across the social scale; from the classy and wealthy in St George's Hill to yer working class in council houses. I bumped into one of the latter working at the Sainsbury checkout. When I got home I found he hadn't charged me for a litre of gin. One widow in her late 70s seemed upset during the funeral, but when I visited two months later she threw open the door and insisted that I had a drink to celebrate that the 'old bugger' had died. He had not talked to her for ten years, and after a silent supper each evening went off to the British Legion club. I asked why she had not left him long ago but she said she had no money and where would she go? At a funeral of a woman who lived in a grace and favour house in Windsor, her son told me that her dog chased a woman on a horse, so mother shouted, 'Come here, Queenie,' which got a very black look from HM.

Once when I told the crematorium lady attendant that the mourners wanted to put rosemary on the coffin she asked, 'Is she heavy?' At Christmas the staff of Hanworth have a raffle, and I was once asked to do the draw. We all stood round behind the scenes eating and drinking whilst every now and again a coffin trundled by. In the midst of life...

2 February 2008. Dame Frances Campbell-Preston, for many years a lady-in-waiting to the Queen Mum, tells me that she tried to retire when she was 80 but Queen Elizabeth told her to keep going, 'My eighties were very happy and so will yours be.' Dame Frances' books are great fun, crammed with amusing stories including: Picasso had died, and David Hockney went to tell Christopher Isherwood who said, 'That's not like him.'

10 February 2008. Have re-started my full-time PhD course. Robert came up with the solution. Why not research the economics of burial in the two cities since 1666? How much and how important were the burial fees to the parishes, and what happened when interments ended in 1852 in the City and Westminster? With Arthur's agreement I went back to vestry minutes, churchwardens' accounts, burial registers etc, and ransacked them to find out. To my amazement I discovered that interment fees accounted for between four and forty-five per cent of parish income (excluding the poor rate).

2 April 2008. Until today I have never met anyone who has actually seen Hitler and Mussolini in the flesh. Luigi Giffone, an architect whose wife's funeral I have taken, tells me on my return visit today that he was a Blackshirt Fascist, and, aged 15, he saw both men at rallies in Rome. His father was mayor of a small town, Tropea, in Calabria, southern Italy, and after the Italians surrendered he was summoned by the local German General because his car had been pelted with tomatoes. Luigi spoke German so went with his father who was told he had 24 hours to find the culprit. When his father went back he said it was probably children and, through Luigi, gave a grovelling apology. The General said he had another 24 hours, then if no name was given he would be tried and shot. His parents had to decide

quickly what to do. However, that very night the Americans bombed and destroyed the German camp which was unsuccessfully camouflaged in the forest. Our friend Raleigh Trevelyan has described these momentous days in his books.[135] At the time he was there as a 21 year old officer; now he is 86, and is a true storyteller we love to be with.

23 April 2008. There is an obituary in *The Times* today of Cardinal Alfonso Trujillo, President of the Pontifical Council for the Family. For two decades this man has pedalled his conservative views against divorce, abortion, contraception and homosexuality. Amongst his horrific views was that condoms couldn't prevent AIDS because the virus was small enough to pass through them, and he reckoned that same-sex couples who adopt are jeopardising the child's future, and that this amounted to an act of moral violence against the child. Good riddance to Trujillo. On the same page as his obit was one for Pushpa Anand, a Hindu guru, whose whole life was devoted to alleviating suffering of families in India. What a contrast.

It is difficult to know which I detest most – conservative Catholics or conservative evangelicals. They resemble a ladies' loo – all clean, bright and sweet smelling, but underneath there is something nasty.

29 April 2008. I wrote to Richard Chartres about a priest having a rough time and got a reply by return. Although I have been retired nearly seven years he is affectionate to me, and we had a good talk at Hanworth where he was presiding at a mass recently. When he arrived as Bishop of Stepney he was a complete contrast to everything we had asked for in the Vacancy in See committee. He had no experience of the Moslem world, and was not known for firm outspoken opinions. Fortunately, probably thanks to his wife Caroline and their children, he soon showed that he had his feet firmly on the ground, and is pastorally sensitive to clergy with problems. Caroline told me that they had one man to stay for a while, and on his first

morning the son came down to breakfast and said, 'Are you having a breakdown?'

Richard seems able to deliver the smuttiest of innuendos with apparent innocence, keeping the humour rude but rarely offensive. Often I have wondered if he realises what he is saying, and yes, he does. At his first huge gathering in the Stepney Area he referred from the pulpit to his predecessor, Jim Thompson. 'You called him Big Jim so I hope you will not know me as Big Dick.' At the Induction of Katharine Rumens, the first woman incumbent in the City, at St Giles, Cripplegate, a large number of women priests were robed and in the sanctuary. Richard, looking at the effigies around the walls of famous parishioners like John Milton and John Speed the mapmaker, climbed into the pulpit and said, 'There are some substantial busts in church tonight.'

Richard looks like a bishop and speaks like one, and people are immensely impressed by him particularly in the City. He dislikes being controversial so keeps silent on most issues, and, although he was in the running for Canterbury, he was not appointed. Very strange, really, as I gather when he was Runcie's chaplain he wrote many of the speeches. He always includes humour and one of his best stories concerned the astrologer of a tabloid newspaper who was taken ill so the editor asked an old hack to do the My Stars column. For Virgo he wrote: 'All the horrors that have happened in your life are as nothing to what will happen to you today.' The switchboard was jammed with calls.

1 May 2008. Last year I orchestrated a campaign to get Donald Reeves an honour for his mediation work in Bosnia – getting former enemies to talk and do practical projects like building a mosque. Prince Charles wrote in support, and the campaign worked, so today I went with Peter, his partner, and Kate to the Palace for the Investiture. We had to be there 45 minutes before kick-off but I wasn't bored for a second. We were in the Ballroom with its two huge gilt thrones under heavily-draped canopies at

one end, and the Irish Guards band on the shelf at the other end playing songs from the shows mixed with Mozart and Bach. We sat on red plush benches facing each other and in between us were rows of gilt chairs facing Ma'am, who first saw in private the family of Captain David Hicks of the Royal Anglian Regiment to give them his posthumous MC. This was my regiment over 50 years ago when I was in the Royal Norfolk's as a subaltern. It then joined the Suffolk Regiment (Snuffolks?), - then it merged with the Essex Regiment. Two other Anglians received an MC today so I felt proud and tearful. In fact I always feel tearful when the Queen is around.

There were 98 recipients today, and she is briefed by an RAF Equerry as each person walks forward. She is a star, and asked how on earth Donald got into the Bosnia business, then pinned an MBE on him. She holds 25 Investitures every year and makes an entrance attended by two Gurkha officers – Queen Victoria started this in 1876. Five Yeomen of the Guard surround her – that dates back to 1485. We had photographs in the Courtyard afterwards, then Robert and Andrew Barr joined us for lunch at the Athenaeum. Andrew writes books about *Songs of Praise*, and sends me hilarious minutes of a spoof cathedral of the Utterly Divided Trinity in the Shires.

5 May 2008. Mark Bowman recorded an interview with me today on behalf of the Lesbian Gay Bisexual and Transgender Religious Archives Network based in the USA. He was courteous and kind to me and just let me talk and answer questions.[136]

10 June 2008. After 30 years Richard Kirker is leaving LGCM, so we lunch at the Garrick. The gay world owes him a huge debt because he has borne the brunt of all the criticisms and abuse. As time has gone by he has changed from being a controversial campaigner to being a diplomat and statesman with gravitas. Fortunately he has kept his sense of humour.

12 July 2008. Salley Vickers' new book *Where Three Roads Meet* describes the last years of Freud and a conversation he had with

a shadowy figure about Oedipus and his father. I've read it twice and the mist is clearing, but I have identified with some of Freud's remarks about the Divinity. 'God is a projection occasioned by the desire to revert to a state of infantile dependency.' Religion is 'a primitive defence against reality.' 'The ambiguity of religious pronouncements encourages a mystification designed to bolster the authority of those who make the pronouncements.' I like these, and in this month of the Lambeth Conference – what a colossal waste of money and time – my faith is draining away. The bishops' obsession with gays and women bishops disgusts me.

1 August 2008. My mother, in her 98th year, has a few marbles left. She is in a retirement home in Great Yarmouth and when her sister Jean, my beloved aunt (86), breezed in and said, 'Come on, Molly, we are going out for a drive and ice cream,' Mother said to the old lady sitting next to her, 'Not would you like to go out, but you are going out.'

11 August 2008. Robert and I have lunch at the Athenaeum with Morton Cohen, the world's expert on Lewis Carroll. We try to meet every year when he is in London, and find him really charming and fun to be with. He says that when elderly friends meet they begin with an organ recital – their state of health. He lives in New York and Puerto Rico and although 86 he is still writing – at present on Carroll's love of the theatre. We asked him if he would get on with him in Heaven, and he thought probably not because Dodgson was a High Tory, a biblical literalist and rather prudish; all the things Mort is not. At present he is angry with a woman academic who is saying that Carroll was more interested in the mothers than their daughters. Mort, who has edited the letters, agrees that Dodgson writes to the women, but the letters are all about the children. Robert is trying to persuade Mort to write his autobiography, particularly as he lived for over 50 years with Dick who died a few years ago.

21 November 2009. This has been our Annus horribilis

because Robert has gone bankrupt because his development company has gone bust due to the credit crunch and legal covenants which cannot be broken. Our house was repossessed (with a bailiff calling to give us three weeks to get out). Our new house in Woking is half the size of the Weybridge one which in turn was half the square footage of Mill Eyot in Shepperton. So we have sold many of our treasures and my private army of 1,100 lead soldiers had to march off to Bonhams.

It has meant that Robert and I have withdrawn from all our friends because we do not want to rehearse the horrors over and over again. It has been a terrible smack as I have never been short of cash and have always owned a house. One of the saddest moments was saying goodbye to Karen who has looked after us for ten years and is the last in a line of ladies who have kept us in order. Occasionally I am overcome with self-pity and depression closes in, usually early in the morning, so I get up and get going. There is only one way to cope: in Churchill's words, 'Keep buggering on.'

Some reactions have been outrageous – 'See how the mighty have fallen' (a priest); 'Someone else will now be able to enjoy your furniture, clocks etc' (an American professor); 'I'm so glad because it means that lovely house will not be redeveloped' (neighbour in Shepperton); and 'Are you selling any paintings cheap?' (a friend). One man said, 'Your faith will help you.' What faith? Others have been immensely kind and offered loans.

Holy Saturday 2010. Roland Macleod usually comes to Sunday lunch with us every month, and this morning I panicked because we had not heard from him, so went to his house in Forest Gate and, as I have his keys, let myself in. He was dead on the bedroom floor which was a huge shock. Feeling terrible I phoned the police who came with an ambulance. They let me say the commendation prayers then took him away. Somehow I got home and collapsed. In the evening the Coroner phoned to ask how I was.

5 May 2010. Roland's funeral at Eltham Crematorium. His nephew from New Zealand played the bagpipes – the lament *Flowers of the Forest*. I take the service and Stanley Baxter gives an amusing eulogy. I shall miss Roland terribly as I have known him since Cuddesdon in 1960. He was not ordained but became an actor, nearly always playing vicar roles. He was in *Coronation Street* and everyone always hailed him, 'Hello Vicar.' I am his only executor so have to clear the house and sell it. Three thousand books await, including some valuable books on horse racing and bloodstock. He had an incredible memory and could tell you all the Derby winners.

21 July 2010. Mother has died in Great Yarmouth, three months short of her 100th birthday. I felt relieved as she has been in a coma for several days. My last conversation with her was memorable because I asked her if she realised her sister Jean was a criminal. I got 'The Look' so explained that Jean had been done for speeding (36 mph). Mother roared with laughter then slipped into unconsciousness. I shall conduct the funeral as I don't want an unknown cleric making mistakes.

5 August 2010. Lunch with Mary Everingham, former St Botolph's caretaker, who asks me to take her funeral. She is now a tiny little thing thanks to many operations, and I asked her how she feels about dying. 'OK, but you feel a bit stiff the next morning.' She is a real East Ender and her family are enabling her to remain in her Bethnal Green flat.[137]

3 November 2010. An old friend of mine in the church tells me that he was in a gay sauna near Marble Arch recently where he was surprised to encounter a leading evangelical, who when they had met previously had expressed strongly homophobic views. He told me that they spoke over a cup of tea, and that the evangelical had commented that he enjoyed having a sauna, and it wasn't necessary to take advantage of everything on offer in such a place. Ho Hum.

5 December 2010. Gordon Gardiner, one of my closest friends,

throws splendid parties stuffed with Dames and Glitterati, and today's birthday celebration at the Garrick was no exception. I was introduced to Lord Browne, and I regret to say I didn't congratulate him for surviving the scandal when he was 'outed' three years ago and had to resign as Chief Executive of BP. Since then he has urged companies to do more to end discrimination against gays. I suspect that his handsome young partner, Nghi, has given him security and support to do this.

14 December 2010. Aged 74 I was doctored today. After nearly five years blood, sweat and research, King's College, London awarded me the degree. When I told people my plans I received much criticism usually along the lines of why should you spend your retirement doing this. 'It will be the last opportunity to humiliate you,' said +Rowan. Fees were a problem – around £4,000 p.a. for a full-time course. All the churchy trusts such as Sion College declined to help because they concentrate their funds on young women and men who have a career ahead of them. Fortunately Peter Scott offered to pay half, and the rest came from ash cash. Andrew Lodge, a director of the famous Surrey undertaking firm, said that he was glad to help, 'We support help the aged.' My good friends Peter Galloway and Julian Litten have given me an enormous amount of advice and encouragement. As they both have doctorates they know what is involved. I was extremely fortunate because Dr Arthur Burns gave me his full attention at our monthly meetings, and his criticisms were always constructive.

I was extremely apprehensive about the viva, and a young friend who had been through the process recently told me, 'I don't think I ate for about two days beforehand I felt so queasy with nerves.' Equally terrified I was ushered into the presence of the Venerable Bill Jacob, Archdeacon of Charing Cross and DJ James, Professor of Pastoral Theology in the University of Wales, Lampeter. With him was Professor Vanessa Harding of the history department at Birkbeck College, London. They quizzed me on my thesis for ninety minutes. I then retired, and when they asked me to return Professor Harding said that my research was impressive and I had passed. I wanted to give her a big kiss, I was so relieved. Arthur uncorked a bottle of sparkling wine to celebrate, and they asked me what the tie was I was wearing. I told them that it was my regimental tie (Royal Norfolk's) because that was the last time I was under fire – Cyprus in 1956.

21 December 2010. My letter in *The Times* today (about bishops, a favourite subject) announced to the world my new status, and letters and e-mails flowed in. One said that I was following another Dr Johnson who was also a man of letters and disgraceful morals. If people hear I am a doctor they usually ask if I could give advice on their haemorrhoids or hernias.

23 December 2010. The stress surrounding the viva had made my body seize up and stiffen with anxiety, and this brought back the stabbing back pain which referred itself down my left leg. Originally it was caused by lifting sacks of Roland's books. I now have to walk with a stick and a few days ago the pain was so severe that Robert had to drive me to Accident/Emergency whose staff dosed me up with tranquillisers. Today I got an urgent appointment with Dr Evans, my GP, who gave me very strong painkillers which he said would relax me so that healing could take place. It is two days before Christmas, and when I collected the pills from the chemist he said, 'You mustn't drink with these.' The other people in the shop said, 'Happy Christmas.'

11 January 2011. A full church for Peter Scott's Memorial Service at St Paul Knightsbridge. I had anointed him before he died then took his funeral and miss him greatly. His son Alex gave a masterly tribute to his complicated father. I arrived early so spent an hour with Richard Coles the former Communard now assistant priest at St Paul's. He was ordained six years ago when he was 43 and is clever, witty and absolutely delightful. His radio broadcasts reach more people than all the clergy put together, and he is a splendid advert for the C of E.

25 March 2011. As Master Emeritus I was invited to the first visit of the Queen as Patron of the Royal Foundation of St Katharine. Her mother visited us every year but obviously that is not possible for her. I debated long and hard whether to go because they gave me the boot. After a short service in chapel I was presented, and when she asked about my time I nearly let the cat out of the bag. Later when we were all standing around to say goodbye I told her that I am lunching with Roger Royle tomorrow. Her face lit up, 'I do very much miss him on the radio in the mornings. That laugh of his is very special.' I can't wait to tell Roger that the secretary of his fan club lives at the end of the Mall.

13 April 2011. Robert and I drive to Hereford for John Hencher's funeral. The other John is devastated having nursed him for many months. +Rowan asked me to read this:

> I valued greatly his friendship and his exceptionally fresh and penetrating spirit. I know how very deeply he was valued as a pastor by generations of students at Monmouth School; but I was also privileged to hear and see something of his personal spiritual discipline and vision. He was a deeply serious priest – as well as a deeply life-enhancing presence; perhaps the two go together in an ideal world! The Church in its present shape was never an easy home for him, and he wrote movingly to me about his increasing sense of finding a home among the Friends. I'm very thankful to have known him and pray for his peace.

18 July 2011. Can anyone find their way around the labyrinthine Barbican Centre? I arrive an hour early for my graduation and collect my hired gear which includes a fetching black velvet dinner-plate hat with tassel; then I find places for my guests Robert, Joy Dawson and Michael. I'm first up and the Principal tells me that he'd like to read my thesis (presumably he suffers

from insomnia). Am particularly pleased that Arthur Burns, my supervisor, is there to support me.

15 October 2011. Hundreds of clergy assemble at Salisbury on a sunny day for Nick Holtam's enthronement as the seventy-eighth Bishop of the diocese. It was a splendid liturgy which included the Asperges when schoolchildren sprinkled us as a reminder of our baptism. Our eight year old arrived with a teacher holding a bowl and sprinkled the floor so I told her she was meant to spray us. Her eyes lit up and we were duly drenched. Nick preached a forceful, challenging sermon and for once my heart lifted in joy at a cathedral service. Joy Dawson, one of my dearest friends, came in style from Bournemouth with Adrian Scott, the Deputy Lieutenant, in his car. She is a retired Chief Cardiac Technician from Great Ormond Street and regularly distinguishes herself by writing pro-gay letters to the press, beginning: 'As a heterosexual 79 year old...'

5 April 2012. Robert and I attend a civil partnership ceremony of a priest friend and his other half. Robert, who now has no Christian faith, is very shocked that on a very important day in this man's life the God whom he worships cannot be mentioned. I agree, and this must surely be the reason for supporting gay marriage and for bishops to allow their clergy discretion to officiate in church. I read in the press that 50,000 same-sex couples have been through the ceremony so far.

15 June 2012. Roger Royle and I have a quiet lunch at the Garrick to mark the 50th anniversary of our deaconing. How has the Church survived us, and how have we survived? He now looks a lot older than me, but then he always has done...

31 July 2012. I conducted the funeral of Eric Sykes at Leatherhead crematorium and reporters were fortunately unobtrusive. The service is for family and close friends as there will be a Memorial Service later. I recognised many of the congregation but had difficulty naming them. My visit to his widow and three daughters was a riot – so much laughter as they remem-

bered him. I hadn't realised he was deaf for most of his life and that his mother died soon after he was born; he always felt her presence close to him. He was very good pals with Spike Milligan whose office was next door to his. On their way to lunch Spike once lay down on the pavement outside an undertakers and shouted 'Shop'. Norma Farnes, the secretary of them both, spoke movingly, and Jimmy Tarbuck described Eric as a man of gentle, never cruel comedy who millions loved. He and Hattie Jacques were a great pair on TV.

Postscript

Now 76, I tend to look down memory lane instead of focusing on the future. Perhaps publishing this diary will help put the past to bed. I shall, however, never recover from St Botolph's homeless work collapsing. The hostels continue and Kipper is flourishing but what happened to the hundreds each day who visited the crypt?

The way people regard LGBT people has changed beyond all recognition over 50 years; who would have imagined a Conservative government backing gay marriage? Sadly it will take away an Anglican priest's discretion to take such a service. However, the place of gays in the Church has not changed; it is a dangerous place to be. Most gay and lesbian clergy still lead closeted lives and to receive preferment one has to be celibate or *say* one is celibate.

Much of what Richard Holloway writes in the latter part of *Leaving Alexandria*[138] resonates, but I do still believe in God although often He seems a Cosmic Sadist. I follow Jesus because his teaching is the only thing that makes sense in this crazy world, and I accept his promise (and it <u>is</u> a promise), that if we want, we shall go with him to the next world after death. I still pray and remember those I love or who are in need, but I do not often attend church because the services are so stunningly boring and wordy. Since the age of ten I have always felt an outsider and still am. Perhaps I should follow my friend John Hencher's example and find a Quaker Meeting House. Father died at 68 and Mother at 99, so perhaps I have a few more years to be with Robert. Derek Harbord sent me a telegram on my induction at St Botolph's in 1974, so perhaps I should now send it to myself:
GAWDELPYER.

Endnotes

1. In 2000, Sister Etheldreda in Belfast heard one of my broadcasts and wrote to ask if I was 'the well-mannered boy whose family lived in Yarmouth.'

2. Founded as Suffolk's memorial to the Prince Consort, and originally known as the Albert Memorial College.

3. LJ Baggott later Archdeacon of Norwich. He retired to Hampshire and came to my ordination in 1962.

4. Today Durham is separated from Newcastle and has 15,000 students in many more colleges.

5. Major-General the Honourable William Herbert, son of the 2nd Earl of Powis.

6. This antique office, which someone said involved a lot of paperwork, dates from 1487 and carries a salary of £7 p.a. He presides over the College of royal chaplains.

7. The Society of the Sacred Mission, founded in 1893, had its motherhouse in Kelham until 1973 when numbers dropped. It is now at Willen, near Milton Keynes.

8. I had invited him to speak to Durham SCM, and liked him enormously. Later he apologised to me for this advice, and said that he was very ignorant about homosexuality in those days. I suspect that he was 100% heterosexual.

9. He became vicar of St Alban, Holborn and is now one of my closest friends.

10. Lysergic Acid Diethylamide is a semisynthetic psychedelic drug which was used in the 1950s and 1960s but is now banned for medical, recreational and spiritual uses.

11. He had been a Bush Brother in Australia for 16 years. He died in 1969.

12. Bruce Carpenter, Chris Sansbury and Edwin Barnes.

13. Cosmo Gordon Lang was vicar of the next-door parish – St Mary, Portsea – then became Bishop of Stepney, Archbishop

of York and in 1928 Archbishop of Canterbury until 1942. An autocrat, he was not immediately likeable and was almost certainly gay. His portrait painter asked, 'Which man shall I paint?'

14. Provost of Portsmouth 1939–1971 when he resigned after a scandal.

15. Twenty-five years later the extension was completed and consecrated.

16. Later Bishop of the Episcopal Diocese of Bethlehem in the States.

17. From 1969 when Gordon became Dean of Llandaff, Eric was Senior Chaplain again until 1990.

18. University College was founded in 1826 by Jeremy Bentham and others with the intention of keeping the Established Church out so all other colleges followed suit except King's, which Bishop Blomfield in response founded three years later as a church college.

19. The Trust was founded in 1958 to complement the Homosexual Law Reform Society. Antony Grey and others provided counselling at the offices in Shaftesbury Avenue.

20. Stopford (1901–1976) had been Bishop of Peterborough before moving to London in 1961. He had a particular interest in education.

21. We did have more serious speakers such as Dame Cicely Saunders, Marghanita Laski, Andrew Cruickshank, Mary Whitehouse and Lord Soper.

22. He had already offered me five central Norwich parishes in 1967.

23. The Metropolitan Church. Its members are mostly gay or lesbian.

24. Like Blomfield, Gerald had been rector of St Botolph, Bishopsgate, Bishop of Chester, then of London.

25. The Rt Revd Ivol Ira Curtis, Bishop of Olympia.

26. Delderfield founded the right-wing New Britain Party in

1977, and for a time was a Common Councilman in the City of London.

27. After a while the Bishop appointed three others including Norry McCurry, rector of Stepney, and the saintly Daphne Jones whom David adores.

28. Rodney gave him an implant and counselling. The man has not used alcohol since, and is now a university lecturer.

29. Strangely enough the incumbent, Peter Clarke, got no criticism for this.

30. The church insurance was increased from £30,000 to £200,000 a few weeks earlier.

31. He was MP for the Isle of Ely 1924–29, then represented Hendon South 1945–70.

32. He died at Morden College, Blackheath in 1998.

33. Now Sanctuary Housing.

34. Runcie on the *Church Times* – 'It's a duty to read it and a sin to enjoy it.'

35. Mary Whitehouse, 1910–2001, founded the National Viewers' and Listeners' Association in 1965 to clean up TV and the media. In 1977 she successfully prosecuted *Gay News* for blasphemous libel and the editor, Dennis Lemmon, received a suspended sentence.

36. Secretary of the Homosexual Law Reform Society 1962–82, and of the Albany Trust, 1958–77.

37. I used a photo of it for my book, *Outside the Gate*.

38. The Collection closed in 1986, and Lydia is back in Yarmouth.

39. Robert Robinson, who painted between 1688 and 1696, depended on travellers' tales so most of the animals are decidedly odd.

40. I heard later that Freddy didn't think that his family Trust would approve. However, he gave a very large grant a few years later to found the Kobler Clinic at Charing Cross Hospital for people affected by AIDS/HIV.

41. It became known as the Gloucester Report because that Bishop was the chairman.

42. The Salvation Army built a new hostel in Whitechapel, which was opened by the Queen in the autumn.

43. I don't think the first two exist, but the others are among the 69 churches in the Square Mile which have been demolished since 1666. Thirty-nine remain.

44. Written by Wynyard Browne, it had been a success on the West End stage.

45. Ellison cared for the troubled diocese of Bermuda for a few years, then he and Jane retired to Cerne Abbas, Dorset. He died 1 October 1992 having been a bishop for 44 years.

46. He was nearer the truth than he realised.

47. It was to be Graham Leonard, Anglo-Catholic, archconservative, and the man who defeated reunion with Methodists *c.* 1969. On *Desert Island Discs* he said that he was totally opposed to the ordination of women – he might be attracted to the celebrant at the Eucharist.

48. Born 1944 and lives in Hemsby, Norfolk.

49. Mayes, 1861–1952 was an RA. My grandfather Delf painted with him in Yarmouth.

50. During his 28 years of service with the Church, he established the largest AIDS service centre in the San Gabriel Valley; supervised the creation of the Young & Healthy Program, which serves uninsured and underinsured children; and established Union Station, a homeless shelter.

51. John Boswell, 1947–94, was a linguistic genius who read more than 15 ancient and modern languages. His second book *Same-Sex Unions in Pre-modern Europe* argued that same-sex union ceremonies had become highly-developed church rituals by the 12th century. He likened these voluntary same-sex unions to heterosexual marriages and argued that they were entered into freely by male couples who desired to celebrate sacramentally their emotional

bond with one another.

52. Professor of the History of the Church at the University of Oxford since 1997, and Fellow (formerly Senior Tutor) of St Cross College, Oxford (since 1995). Though ordained as a deacon in the Church of England, he declined ordination to the priesthood for political reasons. His TV series *History of Christianity* (2009) was very well received.

53. Further charges followed in 2002 and 2006.

54. American organisation for gay Roman Catholics.

55. Her *View Modern Sculpture* is in Fitzroy Square Gardens.

56. Lady Elizabeth, 1908–2000, was the daughter of the 7th Earl of Dartmouth.

57. Barbara published *Vihares and Verandas*, a book of her drawings, in 1978. She has exhibited her drawings and woven panels in Asia, Europe and North America. She founded and has been for thirty years the designer for Barefoot, a company of rural hand weavers in Sri Lanka.

58. Provost of the City Polytechnic.

59. In 1988 he became Director of the Tate Gallery.

60. Leslie Crowther, 1933–1996, was a famous comedian, actor and game show host with his catchphrase, 'Come on down.' He himself had a serious drink problem but after treatment gave it up in 1989.

61. After about a year both Lucas and Watson with their lay representatives returned to Chapter and Synod.

62. Worth £224,000 in 2011.

63. Lord Mayor in 1982.

64. Malcolm Johnson, *Outside the Gate* (1994) pp. 48–9.

65. Sadly there is no such company.

66. He became Dean of Guildford in 2001, and retired in 2012.

67. St Luke's later declined to admit clergy with the virus.

68. He retired in 2006.

69. This is the name given by the Episcopalian Church to its leading incumbents.

70. Cassidy became Bishop of Southwell and Nottingham in 1999.

71. A faculty is a written document issued by the Judge (Chancellor) of a diocese giving permission for a proposed change in the fabric of a church.

72. Founded in 1979 they devote themselves to the expiation of guilt and promotion of joy.

73. He died in 1996 aged 68.

74. I am grateful to Victor Stock who mentions this in *Confessions of a City Priest* (2001) p. 39.

75. Evelyn Garth Moore (1906–1990) was also Chancellor of Durham and Gloucester dioceses. Wise, witty and entertaining, he was also very conservative and once commented that 'a choir of women resplendent in floppy caps and purple, like so many bishopesses, is neither enjoined nor forbidden by the law.'

76. Later Vicar General of the Province of Canterbury and Chancellor of the dioceses of Bath and Wells and Truro.

77. The Catholic Apostolic Church in Gordon Square was opened in 1853 and leased to the Anglican University Chaplaincy 1963–94. The last Apostle died in 1901 but their elders still controlled the use of the building.

78. Probably due to the kindness of Archdeacon Derek Hayward of the London Diocesan Fund I was never asked to pay this sum.

79. Newsome died in 1992.

80. Both men returned a year later. Ian Findlay was chairman of Sedgwick Forbes, our neighbour in Aldgate and chairman of Lloyds. He died on 29 December 2001.

81. James founded the Hampstead Theatre in 1959, and won fame by adapting and directing *84 Charing Cross Road*.

82. Later Bishop of Lynn, then Dean of Windsor.

83. These receptions continued for several years. A book was later placed in Southwark Cathedral.

84. Victor Stock of St Mary-le-Bow, Donald Reeves of St James's Piccadilly, Christopher Hamel Cooke of St Marylebone, Geoffrey Brown of St Martin-in-the-Fields and me. I have the minutes of our meetings.

85. Sadly Ken and Emma divorced in 1994.

86. Later Dean of Salisbury.

87. Later Bishop of Guildford, then Chelmsford.

88. Later Bishop of Thetford.

89. He was chairman of the family firm, Provincial Insurance Company, and a generous benefactor.

90. No meeting took place.

91. £120,000 was received from this ITV Sunday Evening Appeal.

92. CARA was founded by David in 1988 as a community of friendship of people living with HIV. The word Cara is derived from the Gaelic word for friend. In 2012 it is based at 240 Lancaster Road, London W11 4AH.

93. Crisis goes from strength to strength. In 2012 it opened nine centres over the Festival and entertained over 3,000 homeless people.

94. Monsignor Graham Leonard died on 6 January 2010.

95. He had been a parish priest in Old Ford and later went on to be Bishop of Dunwich.

96. In 1997 he was appointed Bishop of Sheffield.

97. Gonville, 1912–91, was expelled from South Africa when as Dean of Johannesburg he attacked apartheid. He was appointed vicar of St Vedast in the City and lived opposite us in Tredegar Square.

98. Prebendary Norman McCurry 1919–93.

99. He died in 1999.

100. Later Bishop of Jarrow, then Lincoln.

101. In 2012 it was merged with the Shepherds Bush Housing Group, so I ceased to be President.

102. Deputy Director of OXFAM.

103. London Lighthouse, Lancaster Road W11 was founded by Andrew Henderson and Christopher Spence in 1986.

104. He died on 11 August 2002.

105. Peter Levene started his career in the defence industry and held a number of government jobs. As chairman and chief executive of Canary Wharf Ltd he rescued them from bankruptcy. He became a Life Peer in 1997, and Chairman of Lloyds of London in 2002.

106. Invitations to Mayoral banquets usually have a slip enclosed, 'Ladies shall wear tiaras'.

107. His sister Rosemary Bailey wrote his biography *Scarlet Ribbons: A Priest with AIDS*.

108. Bennett. He wrote the official biography of King George VI.

109. The others were Andrew Henderson and Liz Waller.

110. The community was founded as a nursing order in 1848, and has done some splendid work as midwives in the East End. As numbers dwindled they moved from Poplar to Bow, and are now in Birmingham.

111. In 2012 Jennifer Worth's TV series based on their work, *Call the Midwife*, captivated the nation.

112. In 2010 he became a Roman Catholic.

113. The London diocese has had several long-standing incumbents – Gordon Taylor at St Giles-in-the-Fields had been there since 1949, Chad Varah at St Stephen Walbrook since 1953, and William Atkins at St George, Hanover Square since 1955.

114. Wife of Sir Richard O'Brien, a war hero who was Montgomery's PA. A devout Anglican, he was later chairman of the Commission on Britain's urban priority areas which produced *Faith in the City*.

115. John was a convinced Christian, totally committed to social and economic progress. He was Director of the Industrial Society 1962–86, and was appointed CBE in 1970.

116. Fiennes died in June 2011.

117. His statue, moved from St Pancras Cemetery, is in the crypt of St Martin's.

118. Bishop of Birmingham.

119. It did. We only had three meetings.

120. Since 1975 he has been a lecturer at St John's College/Cranmer Hall in Durham.

121. This was the first time private soldiers received a medal; till then it was officers only.

122. I met him nine years later, and he had given up this work because he had come to terms with being gay himself.

123. A priest is still preaching – facing the congregation – at his own funeral!

124. This was Disraeli's description of him.

125. John sadly died a few weeks later.

126. Director of Social Services in the City of London. She was a terrific help when I was at St Botolph's.

127. Later I heard from someone present that Livingstone asked what the bishops were doing for the gay community as London is full of gay bars etc. No one spoke, then apparently Tom Butler mouthed platitudes. 'He dug a pit then fell in.'

128. David Brewer whom I first met at Sedgwick's in Aldgate in 1977. He was Lord Mayor 2005/6 and knighted. In 2008 the Queen made him Lord-Lieutenant of Greater London.

129. BBC *Newsnight* interview with Kirsty Wark 17 June 2003.

130. He didn't.

131. Malcolm Campbell, 1885–1948, was a racing motorist and motoring journalist.

132. His son Donald had a similarly named boat which sank after a 300 mph crash in 1967 on Coniston Water.

133. Two years later he still had not bothered to call in.

134. Professor Donald Allchin, Dr George Lovell, Bishop Peter Lee, Ms Madeleine Bunting, Miss Peggy Hartley and Ernest Warrell.

135. Notably *Rome 44: The Battle for the Eternal City* (New Edition 2004).
136. The interview can be heard on Google.
137. Sadly she died (at home) on 5 January 2013.
138. Richard Holloway, *Leaving Alexandria* (2012, Canongate).

Index

As this diary has a cast of thousands only those who are famous, infamous or have had an impact on me are listed below.

CHRISTIAN
ALTERNATIVE

Throughout the two thousand years of Christian tradition there have been, and still are, groups and individuals that exist in the margins and upon the edge of faith. But in Christianity's contrapuntal history it has often been these outcasts and pioneers that have forged contemporary orthodoxy out of former radicalism as belief evolves to engage with and encompass the ever-changing social and scientific realities. Real faith lies not in the comfortable certainties of the Orthodox, but somewhere in a half-glimpsed hinterland on the dirt track to Emmaus, where the Death of God meets the Resurrection, where the supernatural Christ meets the historical Jesus, and where the revolution liberates both the oppressed and the oppressors.

Welcome to Christian Alternative... a space at the edge where the light shines through.